Perfect Pasta

HOME COOKING

© 1994 Time-Life Books B.V.
First published jointly by Time-Life Books B.V. and
Geddes & Grosset Ltd.

Material in this book was first published as part of the series
HEALTHY HOME COOKING.

ISBN 0 7054 2022 1

Printed in Italy.

Perfect Pasta

BY

THE EDITORS OF TIME-LIFE BOOKS

TIME-LIFE BOOKS/GEDDES & GROSSET

Contents

Bravo, Pasta

Pasta is easy, and pasta is cheap. Better yet, it is good for you. It has become the preferred food of many sportsmen and women before a race or match, packing its own wallop of energy. And weight-conscious cooks can delight in the knowledge that pasta is not the fattening food everyone thought it was.

What makes pasta exceptional? Its wheat-flour starch, for one thing. A complex carbohydrate, the starch provides as much energy as pure protein. Moreover, pasta is easy to digest, and it provides a long-lasting feeling of satisfaction that can be a boon to girth-watchers by curtailing their appetites. The wonder is that a food so sustaining should have relatively few calories: 150 g (5 oz) of cooked spaghetti contains a slender 200 calories, less than half those in the equivalent weight of sirloin steak.

Pasta has further advantages. Its protein is made up of six of the eight essential amino acids; for pasta to be a complete food, all it needs is a little meat or grated cheese to round out and enhance its protein. Pasta also contains niacin, thiamine and riboflavin, calcium and iron, and fibre. Sauced wisely and well, a pasta dish served with a fresh green salad, and followed by a fruit dessert, is a perfect meal, high in satisfaction and nutrition.

Pasta's infinite variety

Pasta is traditionally defined as a wheat-paste food made from flour and water, and that definition can be stretched to include Asian noodles, which can be made from rice, mung beans, buckwheat or other ingredients, as well as wheat. The dried commercial variety is generally produced from protein-rich semolina, coarsely ground endosperm of kernels of hard durum wheat. When water is added to semolina flour and the dough is worked, gluten is developed and a resilient dough is formed. The dough is then extruded or stamped out under great pressure by machine, the resulting pasta is carefully dried. Occasionally eggs are added to yield the egg noodles so popular in Central European dishes. Most dried pasta has a long shelf life and can be safely stored in a dry place for up to two years without losing flavour.

While dried pasta is best when made with semolina, fresh pasta can be prepared at home with ordinary flour. In this book fresh pasta recipes call for unbleached strong plain flour, or finely milled semolina combined with the strong plain flour. Fortunately, finely milled semolina is becoming increasingly available in supermarkets (the coarsely milled type absorbs water poorly and is difficult to work with by hand). The recipes tell how much water to add to the dough—but since flours differ in their ability to absorb moisture, more may be used if the dough proves too stiff to roll out easily by hand or through a pasta machine.

Our recipes sing the praises of pasta. Though they concentrate on pasta as a main course, they also present recipes for pasta appetizers and side dishes. The recipes deal with fresh pasta and dried pasta.

Since pasta comes in a dizzying range of sizes and shapes, pages 44-45 illustrate all the types called for in the recipes and identify them by the names under which you are likely to find them in the shops. But the varying names of the shapes of pasta, particularly those from Italy, can be confusing. Names commonly used in northern Italy, for instance, often differ from those in the south, so when buying pasta it is best to look for the shape rather than the name.

In buying dried pasta, examine the label to be certain that the pasta has been produced with semolina. Pastas made with all or part farina, the coarsely ground endosperm of any wheat except durum, should be avoided because they turn pasty during the boiling. When cooked, good pasta can swell to nearly three times its size and possesses a slightly nutty, sweet flavour.

As for cooking, two rules apply: use a lot of boiling water and be sure not to overcook the pasta (box, page 8). While almost all the recipes in this book call for salting the water, the quantity used is less than that required by many other cookery books. Cooks should bear in mind that the salt is highly diluted when adequate water is used and that a relatively small amount of salt is absorbed by the pasta. Leave it out entirely, and the pasta will be insipid, unless coupled with an intensely flavoured sauce. Some cooks find that a little lemon juice in the water makes a fairly good substitute for salt.

The question of portion size

For consistency's sake, this book employs the same standard measure for a single serving as most pasta manufacturers recommend—60 g (2 oz) dried for 150 g (5 oz) cooked. Most people will probably agree that with a food as popular as pasta 150 g (5 oz) constitutes rather scant eating when presented as a main course. Cooks should feel free to prepare and serve as much pasta as they want so long as they take into account the greater calories the larger portion entails and the caloric value of the rest of the meal, as well as that of the remainder of the day's eating.

The recipes for accompanying sauces list fresh ingredients for maximum flavour and nutrition, but because juicy, well-ripened tomatoes are sometimes unavailable, the recipes offer the option of using whole canned tomatoes. Whole tomatoes are preferred to canned puréed or chopped tomatoes as having better flavour; after draining, they can be easily puréed or chopped. A well-made tomato sauce is one of dining's great pleasures, and it should not be degraded by being dusted with inferior pre-grated Parmesan. Freshly grated cheese is in order. Now that pasta is no longer being maligned as a fattening food, it may be enjoyed to the full. But people should guard against raising the calorie count of a dish by going overboard on the sauce—as is all too often the case—or the bread.

Those pasta lovers, the Italians, know how to sauce a pasta well, which means lightly, and since they often consume it as a first course, they see no need for bread. And they know how to eat pasta properly too—with all the relish that this wonderfully varied, yet amazingly simple, food inspires.

How to Cook Pasta

Pasta is easy to cook; yet all too often it emerges soggy and sticky. Only a few steps need to be followed to ensure perfectly cooked pasta every time.
• Use a big pan and lots of water. As the often repeated expression has it, pasta loves to swim.
• Let the water come to a full boil, then add the salt.
• With the water at a full boil, drop in the pasta, a few handfuls at a time; stir it to keep it from sticking.
• Cover the pan so the water can come back to the boil quickly. Then uncover the pot to prevent boiling over, and adjust the heat to maintain a rolling boil.
• Begin timing the pasta once the water has resumed boiling. Test for doneness by biting into a piece of the pasta; when the pasta is *al dente*—that is, just right to the tooth, deliciously chewy without a floury taste—it is ready. Logic dictates that pastas of different thicknesses will take varying times to cook and that fresh pasta, with its higher moisture content, will cook faster than dried. How long a box of pasta has been on the grocer's shelf or on your own can matter too; the older the pasta, the drier it is likely to be and the longer therefore the cooking time. Manufacturers' instructions are not always reliable; the tooth test is safer.
• Drain the pasta at once. Do not rinse it unless the recipe says so (rinsing washes away nutrients).
• Sauce the pasta at once to keep it from sticking to itself and toss it well to distribute the sauce
EDITOR'S NOTE: All recipes for dried and fresh pastas in this book include recommended testing or cooking times in most of the recipes, pasta is cooked according to the following proportions of water and salt:

PASTA	WATER	SALT
125-175g (4-6oz)	*2 litres (3¹/₂ pints)*	*1 tsp*
250-300g (8-10oz)	*3 litres (5 pints)*	*1¹/₂ tsp*
350-500g (12-16oz)	*4 litres (7 pin ts)*	*2 tsp*

The Key to Better Eating

Home Cooking addresses the concerns of today's weight-conscious, health-minded cooks with recipes that take into account guidelines set by nutritionists. The secret of eating well, of course, has to do with maintaining a balance of foods in the diet. The recipes thus should be used thoughtfully, in the context of a day's eating. To make the choice easier, an analysis is given of nutrients in a single serving. The counts for calories, protein, cholesterol, total fat, saturated fat and sodium are approximate.

Interpreting the chart

The chart below gives dietary guidelines for healthy men, women and children. Recommended figures vary from country to country, but the principles are the same everywhere. Here, the average daily amounts of calories and protein are from a report by the UK Department of Health and Social Security; the maximum advisable daily intake of fat is based on guidelines given by the National Advisory Committee on Nutrition Education (NACNE); those for cholesterol and sodium are based on upper limits suggested by the World Health Organization.

The volumes in the Home Cooking series do not purport to be diet books, nor do they focus on health foods. Rather, they express a common-sense approach to cooking that uses salt, sugar, cream, butter and oil in moderation while employing other ingredients that also provide flavour and satisfaction. The portions themselves are modest in size.

The recipes make few unusual demands. Naturally they call for fresh ingredients, offering substitutes when these are unavailable. (The substitute is not calculated in the nutrient analysis, however.) Most of the ingredients can be found in any well-stocked supermarket.

Heavy-bottomed pots and pans are recommended to guard against burning whenever a small amount of oil is used and where there is danger of the food adhering to the hot surface, but non-stick pans can be utilized as well. Both safflower oil and virgin olive oil are favoured for sautéing. Safflower oil was chosen because it is the most highly polyunsaturated vegetable fat available in supermarkets, and polyunsaturated fats reduce blood cholesterol; if unobtainable, use sunflower oil, also high in polyunsaturated fats. Virgin olive oil is used because it has a fine fruity flavour lacking in the lesser grade known as "pure". In addition, it is—like all olive oil—high in mono unsaturated fats, which are thought not to increase blood cholesterol. When virgin olive oil is unavailable, or when its flavour is not essential to the success of the dish, "pure" may be used.

About cooking times

To help planning, time is taken into account in the recipes. While recognizing that everyone cooks at a different speed and that stoves and ovens differ, approximate "working" and "total" times are provided. Working time stands for the minutes actively spent on preparation; total time includes unattended cooking time, as well as time devoted to marinating, steeping or soaking ingredients. Since the recipes emphasize fresh foods, they may take a bit longer to prepare than "quick and easy" dishes that call for canned or packaged products, but the difference in flavour, and often in nutrition, should compensate for the little extra time involved.

Recommended Dietary Guidelines

Average Daily Intake		Maximum Daily Intake					
		Calories	Protein grams	Cholesterol milligrams	Total fat grams	Saturated fat grams	Sodium milligrams
Females	7-8	1900	47	300	80	32	2000*
	9-11	2050	51	300	77	35	2000
	12-17	2150	53	300	81	36	2000
	18-54	2150	54	300	81	36	2000
	54-74	1900	47	300	72	32	2000
Males	7-8	1980	49	300	80	33	2000
	9-11	2280	57	300	77	38	2000
	12-14	2640	66	300	99	44	2000
	15-17	2880	72	300	108	48	2000
	18-34	2900	72	300	109	48	2000
	35-64	2750	69	300	104	35	2000
	65-74	2400	60	300	91	40	2000

* (or 5g salt)

*Nests of home-made pasta demonstrate the variety achieved when ingredients as diverse ι
mato and spinach as added to the dough*

The Fun of Making Your Own

One of the pleasures of fresh pasta is making it yourself. You can experiment with a variety of shapes—perhaps even inventing your own—and you can add different flavours and colourful vegetable purées to the dough to please both palate and eye. Photographs on the following pages will show you how.

This section examines fresh pasta's many possibilities—as a starter, main course or side dish. The accompanying sauces, although created to go with a particular pasta, could as easily complement another fresh pasta or a dried pasta of a corresponding shape.

The difference between fresh and dried pasta lies not just in the freshness of the product but in the kinds of flour used. Most dried pastas are held together by the high gluten content of the semolina dough with which they are made. In this section pasta is prepared with unbleached strong plain flour and eggs or with a mixture of finely milled semolina and unbleached strong plain flour. One recipe also includes buckwheat flour, which, despite its name contains no wheat at all; it consists instead of the ground seeds of the flowering buckwheat plant.

Recipes for fresh pasta doughs usually call for two eggs with 175 g (6 oz) of flour. However to keep down the cholesterol in the dough, an egg white is substituted for one of the whole eggs. The recipes using semolina have no eggs at all.

Home-made pasta can be refrigerated for 24 hours when covered with plastic film, or the pasta can be frozen. It is rarely so good, however, as when it is eaten soon after being made. Since it has a relatively high moisture content, it need not be cooked long. And this has the advantage of allowing the ingredients with which some of the doughs have been coloured—from spinach and tomatoes to carrots, beetroot and curry—to shine through undiminished.

Using a Pasta Machine

Making fresh pasta is greatly simplified when a good pasta machine takes over the job that otherwise would have to be done entirely by hand. You can quickly turn out noodles, or sheets of dough that may be cut and twisted into fancy shapes, such as bow ties, or used for ravioli and tortellini . Photographs on these two pages demonstrate the preparation of the basic dough.

The trick is to roll out the dough repeatedly: it should have a sheen and be satiny to the touch when ready. If the dough gets sticky, flour it well on both sides before running it through again.

You can cook the pasta immediately, or you can reserve all or part of it for later use. To dry it, hang the strands over a pasta drying rack or twist the strands loosely into 'nests' on a lightly floured surface. When the pasta is thoroughly dry, store it in airtight containers.

To freeze fresh pasta, let it dry for 15 minutes or so. Then coil handfuls into nests of serving portion size and place these on a tray. Put the tray in the freezer for an hour; the stiffened pasta can then be stored in heavy-duty polythene bags in the freezer. To cook frozen pasta, put it directly into boiling water, without thawing.

1 ADDING EGG AND OIL TO FLOUR. Place 175g (6 oz) flour in a mixing bowl and make a well in the centre. Drop one whole egg and one egg white into the well, then add 1 tablespoon of oil. (Alternatively, the dough can be prepared in a food processor following directions for basic pasta dough on page 15).

2 BLENDING THE INGREDIENTS. With a wooden spoon or a fork, break the yolk and mix it together with the whites and oil. Then broaden your strokes to incorporate the flour, and continue to mix until all the liquid is absorbed and the dough can be gathered into a ball, adding more flour if necessary.

3 KNEADING BY HAND. Divide the dough into thirds. Cover two of the pieces with plastic film or a bowl to keep them from drying out. On a lightly floured work surface— preferably wood or marble— knead the third piece for several minutes. If the dough feels tough and inelastic, cover it and let it rest for 15 minutes.

4 KNEADING BY MACHINE. Flatten the dough to about 2.5cm (1 inch) thickness and lightly flour both sides. Adjust the pasta machine's smooth rollers for the widest setting. Pass the dough through the feeder, cranking the rollers with one hand and catching the dough with the other as it is extruded.

5 FOLDING THE ROLLED DOUGH. On a lightly floured surface, fold the piece into thirds and press it down to flatten it; then run it lengthwise through the machine once more. Repeat the process six to eight times, folding the dough into thirds each time. In the end, the surface should be smooth and satiny.

6 REDUCING THE THICKNESS. Adjust the control to the next smaller setting, and feed the entire sheet through the machine, without folding. Repeat procedure, narrowing the setting each time, until the desired thickness is achieved —usually with the next-to-last setting. Flour the dough as necessary to prevent sticking, and support the sheet with your free hand to keep it as extended and flat as possible going into and coming out of the rollers.

7 CUTTING NOODLES. With a knife, cut the sheet of dough in half for easier manageability. Flour the strips lightly on both sides and allow them to rest for 10 to 15 minutes before handling them again. Then run one piece of dough at a time through the selected cutting rollers. Gently toss the noodles in flour and set them aside before cutting the next sheet. Repeat the procedures with the remaining sheets of dough.

Mushroom-Stuffed Triangles

Serves 6 as an appetizer

Working (and total) time: about 50 minutes

Calories 265, Protein 10g, Cholesterol 60mg, Total fat 8g,
Saturated fat 3g, Sodium 290mg

	basic semolina pasta dough (opposite)
15 g/¹/₂ oz	dried wild mushrooms, preferably ceps, soaked for 20 minutes in enough boiling water to cover them
250 g/8 oz	fresh mushrooms, wiped clean and finely chopped
2	large shallots, finely chopped
3	garlic cloves, finely chopped
2 tbsp	balsamic vinegar, or 1 tbsp red wine vinegar
4 tbsp	red wine
¹/₄ tsp	salt
	freshly ground black pepper
2 tbsp	fresh breadcrumbs
1.25 kg/2¹/₂ lb	ripe tomatoes, skinned, seeded and chopped, or 800 g (28 oz) canned whole tomatoes, drained and chopped
1	large onion, chopped
3	carrots (about 250 g/8 oz), peeled and chopped
3 tbsp	double cream
40 g/1¹/₂ oz	Parmesan cheese, freshly grated

To make the filling, drain the wild mushrooms, reserving their liquid. Finely chop them and transfer them to a large, heavy frying pan. Add the fresh mushrooms, shallots and two thirds of the garlic. Pour in the reserved mushroom-soaking liquid and bring the liquid to the boil over medium-high heat. Cook the mixture until nearly all the liquid has evaporated—about 5 minutes. Add the vinegar, wine, half of the salt and a generous grinding of pepper. Continue cooking, stirring constantly, until all the liquid has boiled away—about 3 minutes more. Stir in the breadcrumbs and set the mixture aside to cool.

To make the sauce, combine the tomatoes, onion, carrots, some pepper, the remaining garlic and the remaining salt in a saucepan. Add 4 tablespoons of water and bring the liquid to the boil. Cook the mixture until the vegetables are soft and very little of the liquid remains—about 20 minutes. Purée the sauce in a food processor or blender and return it to the saucepan.

Stir in the cream and set the pan aside. Meanwhile, prepare the triangles. First divide the pasta dough into four portions. Cover three of the portions with plastic film or an inverted bowl to keep them from drying out. Roll out the fourth portion to form a long strip about 12.5 cm (5 inches) wide and about 1 mm ($^1/_{16}$ inch) thick *(pages 12-13)*. Cut across the dough at 12.5 cm (5 inch) intervals to form squares, then cut each of the squares into four smaller ones.

Mound about 1 teaspoon of the filling in the centre of a square. Moisten the edges of two adjacent sides of the square. Fold the moistened edges over the filling to form a triangle, and press the edges closed. Repeat the process with the remaining dough and filling.

Add the filled pasta triangles to 3 litres (5 pints) of boiling water with 1$^1/_2$ teaspoons of salt. Start testing the triangles after 1 minute and cook them until they are *al dente*.

Reheat the sauce over medium-high heat; if the sauce is too thick to pour easily, add 1 to 2 tablespoons of the pasta-cooking water. Drain the triangles and transfer them to a serving dish, then pour the warmed sauce over them. Serve immediately; pass the Parmesan cheese separately.

Semolina Pasta Dough

Calories 230, Protein 7g, Cholesterol 0mg, Total fat 1g,
Saturated fat 0g, Sodium 5mg

125 g/4 oz *strong plain flour*
150 g/5 oz *fine semolina*

To prepare the dough in a food processor, first blend the flour and semolina together, then gradually mix in up to 15 cl ($^1/_4$ pint) of water until the mixture just forms a ball. If the mixture is wet to the touch, blend in flour by the tablespoon until the dough feels soft but not sticky. If the mixture does not form a ball, try pinching it together with your fingers. If it is still too dry to work with, blend in water by the teaspoon until the dough just forms a ball. If you have a pasta machine, the dough may be immediately kneaded and rolled out *(pages 12-13)*.

To prepare the dough by hand, blend the flour and semolina in a bowl and make a well in the centre. With a fork or a wooden spoon, gradually mix in up to 15 cl ($^1/_4$ pint) of water until the dough can be pressed together into a solid ball. Transfer the dough to a lightly floured surface and knead it for a few minutes. The dough should come cleanly away from the surface; if it is too wet, incorporate flour a tablespoon at a time until the dough is no longer sticky. If the dough feels dry and crumbly, incorporate water by the teaspoon until it is pliable. Continue kneading until the dough is smooth and elastic—about 10 minutes; alternatively, knead the dough in a pasta machine *(pages 12-13)*.

If you are not using a pasta machine, wrap the dough in greaseproof paper or plastic film and let it rest for 15 minutes before rolling it out.

Basic Pasta Dough

Calories 205, Protein 7g, Cholesterol 60mg, Total fat 7g,
Saturated fat 1g, Sodium 30mg

175–200 g
6–7 oz *strong plain flour*
1 *egg*
1 *egg white*
1 tbsp *safflower oil*

To prepare the dough in a food processor, put 175 g (6 oz) of the flour, the egg, egg white and oil in the bowl of the machine and process the mixture for about 30 seconds If the mixture forms a ball immediately and is wet to the touch, mix in flour by the tablespoon until the dough feels soft but not sticky. If the mixture does not form a ball, try pinching it together with your fingers. If it is still too dry to work with, blend in water by the teaspoon until the dough just forms a ball. If you have a pasta machine, the dough may be immediately kneaded and rolled out *(pages 12-13)*.

To prepare the dough by hand, put 175 g (6 oz) of the flour into a mixing bowl and make a well in the centre. Add the egg, egg white and oil to the well and stir them with a fork or wooden spoon, gradually mixing in the flour. Transfer the dough to a lightly floured surface and knead it for a few minutes. The dough should come cleanly away from the surface; if it is too wet, add flour by the tablespoon until the dough is no longer sticky. If the dough is too dry and crumbly to work with, add water by the teaspoon until it is pliable. Continue kneading the dough until it is smooth and elastic—about 10 minutes; alternatively, knead the dough in a pasta machine *(pages 12-13)*.

If you are not using a pasta machine, wrap the dough in greaseproof paper or plastic film and let it rest for 15 minutes before rolling it out.

EDITOR'S NOTE: In a traditional pasta dough, two eggs are used with 175 g (6 oz) of flour. Here, to reduce the amount of cholesterol in the dough, an egg white has been substituted for one of the whole eggs.

Fettuccine with Swordfish and Roasted Red Pepper

Serves 4

Working (and total) time: about 1 hour

Calories 375, Protein 24g, Cholesterol 100mg, Total fat 15g, Saturated fat 2g, Sodium 215mg

basic pasta dough (page 15)
350g/12oz swordfish or fresh tuna steak, trimmed and cut into 1 cm (¼ inch) cubes
2 garlic cloves, finely chopped
1 tbsp fresh lemon juice
2 tbsp virgin olive oil
1 sweet red pepper
2 tbsp chopped parsley

In an ovenproof baking dish, combine the swordfish cubes, garlic, lemon juice and 1 tablespoon of the oil. Toss well, cover, and let the mixture marinate in the refrigerator for at least 30 minutes.

Roll out the dough and cut it into fettuccine (pages 12-13). Set the pasta aside while you prepare the fish and red pepper.

Grill the red pepper under a preheated grill, about 5 cm (2 inches) below the heat source, turning the pepper from time to time until it is charred on all sides. Transfer the pepper to a bowl and cover the bowl with plastic film, or put the pepper in a paper bag and fold it shut; the trapped steam will loosen the skin. Peel, seed and derib the pepper, holding it over the bowl to catch any juice. Cut it into thin strips and strain the juice to remove any seeds. Set the strips and juice aside.

Preheat the oven to 200°C (400°F or Mark 6). Bake the swordfish cubes in their marinade until they are cooked through—6 to 8 minutes.

Meanwhile, add the fettuccine to 3 litres (5 pints) of boiling water with 1 ½ teaspoons of salt. Start testing the pasta after 1 minute and cook it until it is al dente. Drain the pasta and transfer it to a large bowl. Add the remaining tablespoon of oil, the red pepper and juice and the parsley; toss well. Add the swordfish and its cooking liquid, toss gently, and serve at once.

Tagliarini with Prawns and Scallops

Serves 8

Working (and total) time: about 45 minutes

Calories 380, Protein 23g, Cholesterol 155mg, Total fat 12g, Saturated fat 3g, Sodium 480mg

basic pasta dough (page 15)
spinach pasta dough (page 29)
500 g/1 lb shelled scallops
30 g/1 oz unsalted butter
3 tbsp finely chopped shallot
500 g/1 lb Mediterranean prawns, shelled and deveined, the shells reserved
¼ litre/8 fl oz dry vermouth
small bay leaf
2 tbsp safflower oil
2 tbsp cut fresh chives
¼ tsp salt
white pepper

Roll out the pasta doughs and cut them into tagliarini—very thin noodles (pages 12-13). Set the tagliarini aside while you prepare the prawn and scallop sauce.

Pull off and reserve the firm, small muscle, if there is one, from the side of each scallop. Rinse the scallops, pat them dry, and set them aside. Melt the butter in a heavy-bottomed saucepan over medium heat. Stir in the shallots and cook them until they are translucent—about 2 minutes. Add the reserved prawn shells and any reserved side muscles from the scallops; cook, stirring, for 1 minute. Pour in the vermouth and simmer the mixture for 1 minute more.

Add the bay leaf and 35 cl (12 fl oz) of water to the saucepan. Bring the liquid to the boil. Reduce the heat and simmer the liquid until it is reduced by about half—10 to 12 minutes. Set the pan aside.

To prepare the seafood, heat the oil in a large, deep, heavy frying pan over medium-high heat. Add the prawns and scallops, and saute them for 1½ to 2 minutes, turning the pieces frequently with a spoon. Push the seafood to one side of the pan and strain the liquid from the saucepan into the frying pan. Set the frying pan aside.

Add the tagliarini to 6 litres (10 pints) of boiling water with 3 teaspoons of salt. Start testing the tagliarini after 1 minute and cook it until it is *al dente*. Drain the pasta and add it to the frying pan with the seafood. Season with the chives, salt and some pepper, and toss gently to distribute the prawns and scallops through the pasta. Cover the pan and place it over medium heat to warm the mixture thoroughly—about 1 minute. Serve the tagliarini at once.

Parsley-Stuffed Mini-Ravioli

Serves 6

Working (and total) time: about 1 hour

Calories 215, Protein 12g, Cholesterol 10mg, Total fat 4g,
Saturated fat 2g, Sodium 330mg

	semolina pasta dough (page 15)
125 g/4 oz	*low-fat ricotta cheese*
125 g/4 oz	*low-fat cottage cheese*
125 g/4 oz	*parsley leaves, finely chopped*
30 g/1 oz	*Parmesan cheese, freshly grated*
¹/₄ tsp	*grated nutmeg*
¹/₈ tsp	*salt*
	freshly ground black pepper
12 5 cl/4 fl oz	*skimmed milk*

To prepare the filling, work the ricotta and cottage cheese through a sieve into a bowl. Stir in the parsley, Parmesan cheese, nutmeg, salt and some pepper. Set the mixture aside.

Roll out the dough. Then, following the steps shown below, form it into ravioli that are each about 4 cm/ 1¹/₂ inches) square with ¹/₂ teaspoon of filling inside. Use only about half of the filling to stuff the squares.

To make the sauce, put the remaining filling in a pan over medium-high heat and stir in the milk. Cook the sauce until it is hot but not boiling—about 5 minutes. Keep the sauce warm while you cook the ravioli.

Add the ravioli to 3 litres (5 pints) of boiling wate with 1¹/₂ teaspoons of salt. Start testing the ravioli a ter 1 minute and cook them until they are *al dent* then drain them. Pour the sauce over the ravioli an serve the dish immediately.

Making Ravioli

1 ADDING THE FILLING. Spread the rolled dough sheet on a lightly floured surface. Place dollops of the filling on half of the sheet, taking care to space them evenly, about 2.5 cm (1 inch) apart.

2 COVERING THE FILLING. Brush the other half of the sheet lightly with water. Then fold it gently over the mounds of filling, matching the edges as closely as possible.

3 CUTTING THE RAVIOLI. Startir from the folded edge, use your fr gers or the side of your hand to fore out the air between the mounds filling and to seal the dough. Then ct out the ravioli with a fluted past wheel.

Pressed-Leaf Ravioli in Shallot Butter

Serves 6 as a side dish or first course
Working (and total) time: about 45 minutes
Calories 175, Protein 5g, Cholesterol 55mg, Total fat 8g,
Saturated fat 3g, Sodium 110mg

	basic pasta dough or basic semolina dough *(page 15)*
30 g/1 oz	*combined flat-leaf parsley, dill and celery leaves, stems removed*
30 g/1 oz	*unsalted butter*
1 tbsp	*finely chopped shallot*
1/4 tsp	*salt*
	freshly ground black pepper

Divide the dough into three pieces. Cover two of the pieces with plastic film or an inverted bowl to keep them from drying out, and roll out the third piece into a sheet about 1 mm (1/16 inch) thick *(pages 12-13)*.

Place the pasta sheet on a lightly floured surface. Distribute one third of the leaves over half of the sheet so that they are about 1 cm (1/2 inch) apart. Carefully flatten each leaf in place. Lightly brush the uncovered half of the sheet with water and fold it over the leaves

as shown below. Press the dough down firmly to seal the leaves in, forcing out any air bubbles.

Pass the folded sheet through the pasta machine to obtain a thickness of about 1 mm (1/16 inch). With a large, sharp, chef's knife, cut the sheet into 5 cm (2 inch) squares. Set the squares aside and repeat the process with the remaining dough and leaves.

Melt the butter in a large, heavy frying pan over medium-high heat. Add the shallot and salt, and saute the shallot until it turns translucent—about 2 minutes. Remove the pan from the heat.

Add the ravioli to 3 litres (5 pints) of boiling water with 1 1/2 teaspoons of salt. Start testing the ravioli after 2 minutes and cook them until they are *al dente*. Drain the ravioli and add them to the frying pan with the shallot butter. Shake the pan gently to coat the pasta with the butter. Sprinkle on some pepper and serve hot.

EDITOR'S NOTE: These ravioli make an excellent accompaniment to grilled lamb or veal chops. They may also be served without the shallot butter in a clear consomme.

Cover the pan tightly; simmer the mixture, stirring once after 4 minutes, until all of the liquid is absorbed and the buckwheat groats are tender—about 6 minutes.

Meanwhile, drop the bow ties into 2 litres (3½ pints) of boiling water with 1 teaspoon of salt. Start testing the bow ties after 1 minute and cook them until they are *al dente*. Drain the bow ties and add them to the buckwheat mixture. Stir gently and serve hot.

EDITOR'S NOTE: To intensify the flavours of the dish, prepare it a day in advance and refrigerate it. Reheat it in a shallow baking dish in a preheated 180°C (350° or Mark 4) oven for 10 minutes, or microwave it on high for 90 seconds.

Bow Ties with Buckwheat and Onions

Serves 4

Working (and total) time: about 45 minutes

Calories 210, Protein 6g, Cholesterol 15mg, Total fat 7g, Saturated fat 4g, Sodium 260mg

	semolina pasta dough (page 15, but halve ingredients)
30 g/1 oz	*unsalted butter*
90 g/3 oz	*onion, chopped*
	freshly ground black pepper
100 g/3½ oz	*toasted cracked buckwheat groats (kasha)*
1	*egg white*
¼ tsp	*salt*
17.5 cl/6 fl oz	*unsalted chicken stock*

Cut the dough in half; cover one of the halves with plastic film or an inverted bowl to keep it moist. Roll out the other half into a long rectangle about 1 mm (⅙ inch) thick (*pages 12-13*). Following the steps demonstrated on the right, cut the rectangle into strips and form the strips into bow ties. Repeat the process to fashion bow ties from the other piece of dough.

Melt the butter in a saucepan over medium heat. Add the onion and some pepper; cook for 5 minutes, stirring occasionally. Meanwhile, put the buckwheat groats in a bowl with the egg white and blend well, then add the mixture to the saucepan Increase the heat to high and cook, stirring constantly with a fork, until the mixture is light and fluffy—3 to 4 minutes. Add the salt and stock, then reduce the heat to low.

Shaping Bow Ties

1 CUTTING OUT THE TIES. With a fluted pastry wheel a knife, trim the edges of the rolled dough sheet on flour-dusted surface. Divide the sheet down the midd. Then cut the strips into 2.5 cm (1 inch) widths.

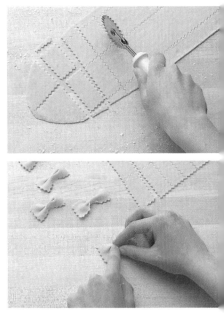

2 TYING THE 'KNOT'. Separate the pieces. Pinch the centre of each between your thumb and forefinger to form bows, holding down the "knot" with the index finger your other hand.

Butternut Agnolotti

Serves 6 as a side dish or appetizer
Working time: about 30 minutes
Total time: about 1 hour and 15 minutes
Calories 335, Protein 9g, Cholesterol 55mg, Total fat 12g,
Saturated fat 3g, Sodium 325mg

	basic pasta dough (page 15)
1	butternut squash (about 500 g/1 lb) halved lengthwise and seeded
35 cl/12 fl oz	unsalted chicken stock
2 tbsp	finely cut chives
45 g/1½ oz	walnuts, finely chopped
1 tbsp	finely chopped fresh sage, or 1 tsp dried sage
½ tsp	salt
¼ tsp	white pepper
30 g/1 oz	unsalted butter
2 tbsp	finely chopped shallots
2 tbsp	flour
4 tbsp	sweet sherry
45 g/1½ oz	raisins
45 g/1½ oz	sultanas

Preheat the oven to 200°C (400°F or Mark 4). Place the squash halves, cut sides up, on a lightly oiled baking sheet; bake them until they are soft—about 1 hour. Allow the squash to cool, then scoop out the pulp and put it in a food processor or blender with 1 tablespoon of the stock. Purée the mixture and transfer it to a bowl. Stir in the chives, walnuts, sage, half the salt and half the pepper.

Divide the dough into three pieces and set two aside, covered with an inverted bowl or plastic film. Roll out the third piece to a thickness of about 1 mm (¹/₁₆ inch). Using a 7.5 cm (3 inch) cutter, cut it into about 12 circles. Roll out and cut the other two pieces. Place 1 teaspoon of filling near the centre of each circle. Lightly brush the edges with water, then fold in half, pressing gently on the edges to seal in the filling.

Melt the butter in a heavy-bottomed saucepan over medium heat. Add the shallots and cook until translucent—about 2 minutes. Stir in the flour and cook, stirring, for 1 minute. Whisk in the remaining stock and the sherry, and continue cooking, whisking constantly, until the sauce thickens and turns smooth—about 1 minute more. Add the raisins and sultanas, reduce the heat to low and simmer for 3 minutes. Season with the remaining salt and pepper.

Cook the agnolotti in 3 litres (5 pints) of gently boiling water with 1½ teaspoons of salt. (If necessary to avoid overcrowding, cook the pasta in several batches.) Start testing the agnolotti after 2 minutes and cook them until they are al dente. With a slotted spoon, transfer them to a warmed, lightly buttered platter. Spoon the sauce over the agnolotti and serve warm.

EDITOR'S NOTE: Pumpkin can be used instead of the butternut squash in this recipe.

Tortellini Stuffed with Veal

Serves 6

Working (and total) time: about 1 hour

Calories 310, Protein 16g, Cholesterol 70mg, Total fat 13g, Saturated fat 4g, Sodium 360mg

	basic pasta dough (page 15)
2 tbsp	virgin olive oil
1	onion, finely chopped
1	carrot, peeled and finely chopped
1	stick celery, finely chopped
4	garlic cloves, very finely chopped
250g/8oz	veal, minced
¼ tsp	salt
	freshly ground black pepper
1 litre/1¾ pints	unsalted chicken stock
4 tbsp	Marsala
2 tbsp	tomato paste
¼ tsp	grated nutmeg
4 tbsp	freshly grated Parmesan cheese
2 tbsp	chopped parsley

Heat the oil in a large frying pan over medium-high heat. Add the onion, carrot, celery and garlic, and cook them, stirring often, until the onion is translucent—about 4 minutes. Add the veal and continue cooking turning the mixture frequently with a spatula or wooden spoon, until the veal is no longer pink—about 5 minutes. Add the salt and some pepper, ¼ litre (8 fl oz) of the stock, the Marsala and the tomato paste. Cover the pan, reduce the heat to medium, and cook for 30 minutes. Remove the pan from the heat and stir in the nutmeg and half of the cheese.

To prepare the pasta, roll out the dough (pages 12 13) and form it into tortellini (right), using 1 teaspoon of the veal mixture to fill each circle. Set the tortellini aside.

To make the sauce, reduce the remaining ¾ litre (1¼ pints) of stock by one third over high heat—about 5 minutes. Stir in the parsley and keep the sauce warm.

Add the tortellini to 3 litres (5 pints) of boiling water with 1½ teaspoons of salt. Start testing the tortellini 2 to 3 minutes after the water returns to the boil and cook them until they are al dente. Drain the pasta and transfer it to a bowl. Pour the sauce over the tortellini and pass the remaining 2 tablespoons of Parmesan cheese separately.

Shaping the Tortellini

FILLING THE TORTELLINI. With a 6 to 7.5 cm (2¹/₂ to 3 inch) pastry cutter, cut circles from the dough. Stack them or store them under a bowl to keep them from drying out. Place some filling on a circle then moisten half the edge with water.

2 ENCLOSING THE FILLING. Fold the circle in half so that the moist and dry edges meet . Press the edges firmly shut to seal them.

3 JOINING THE ENDS. Curl the ends round the filling and pinch these together, moistening the inner surfaces, if necessary, to make them stick. Repeat the steps with the remaining circles.

Tortellini Stuffed with Escargots

Serves 2 (about 24 tortellini)
Working (and total) time: about 45 minutes
Calories 370, Protein 16g, Cholesterol 120mg, Total fat 13g, Saturated fat 8g, Sodium 350mg

	basic semolina pasta dough (page 15, but halve ingredients)
15 g/¹/₂ oz	unsalted butter
1 tbsp	very finely chopped onion
1	garlic clove, very finely chopped
12	giant canned snails (escargots), drained and cut in half (about 125 g/4 oz)
2 tsp	fresh lemon juice
¹/₂ tsp	chopped fresh thyme, or ¹/₄ tsp dried thyme
¹/₈ tsp	salt
	freshly ground black pepper
3 tbsp	finely chopped parsley
4 tbsp	single cream

Melt the butter in a heavy frying pan over medium heat. Add the onion and garlic and cook them, stirring often, for 3 minutes Add the snails, lemon juice, thyme, salt and some pepper; cook for 3 minutes more, stirring frequently. Stir in the parsley and remove the pan from the heat. Transfer the snails to a small dish and refrigerate them. Stir the cream into the pan juices and set aside.

Cut the dough into two pieces. Cover one with plastic film or an inverted bowl to keep it moist. Roll out the other into a sheet about 1 mm (¹/₁₆ inch) thick (pages 12-13). With a 7.5 cm (3 inch) pastry cutter, cut the sheet into 12 circles. Place a snail half slightly off centre on one of the circles Form the round of dough into the shape of a tortellini as demonstrated above. Repeat the process with the remaining dough rounds and then with the other piece of dough.

Cook the tortellini in 3 litres (5 pints) of boiling water with 1¹/₂ teaspoons of salt until they float to the top and are al dente—4 to 5 minutes. Meanwhile, heat the sauce in the frying pan. Drain the tortellini, toss them with the sauce, and serve immediately.

Fettuccine with Oysters, Spinach and Fennel

Serves 4

Working (and total) time: about 1 hour

Calories 420, Protein 22g, Cholesterol 140mg, Total fat
14g, Saturated fat 5g, Sodium 275mg

	basic pasta dough (page 15)
30 g/1 oz	unsalted butter
1	fennel bulb, trimmed, cored and thinly sliced
4	spring onions, trimmed and thinly sliced
500 g/1 lb	fresh spinach, washed and stemmed
1	shallot, finely chopped
12.5 cl/4 fl oz	dry white wine
1 tbsp	chopped fresh tarragon, or 1 tsp dried tarragon
16	oysters, shucked and drained, the liquid reserved (about 15 cl/¹/₄ pint)

Roll out the dough and cut it into narrow fettuccine *(pages 12-13)*. Set the fettuccine aside while you prepare the sauce.

In a heavy frying pan over medium-low heat, melt half the butter. Add the fennel and spring onions cover, and cook until tender—about 10 minutes.

Meanwhile, blanch the spinach in 3 litres (5 pints) of boiling water for 40 seconds. Drain the spinach and refresh it under cold water. Squeeze the spinach dry and separate the leaves. When the fennel and spring onions finish cooking, add the spinach leaves to the pan and remove it from the heat.

In a small saucepan, combine the shallot, wine and half of the tarragon. Cook the mixture over medium-high heat until the liquid is reduced by half—about 5 minutes. Add the reserved oyster liquid and bring it to a simmer—about 3 minutes. Add the oysters to the pan and cook them just until their edges begin to curl—about 2 minutes. Reduce the heat to low to keep the oysters warm.

Cook the fettuccine in 3 litres (5 pints) of boiling water with 1¹/₂ teaspoons of salt. Start testing the pasta after 1 minute and cook it until it is *al dente*. Drain the pasta and transfer it to a large bowl. Swirl the remaining butter into the oyster sauce and combine the sauce with the pasta. Reheat the vegetables in the frying pan and stir in the remaining tarragon, then add the vegetables to the pasta and oyster sauce. Toss well and serve immediately.

Beetroot Ravioli in Soured Cream and Chive Sauce

Serves 6
Working time: about 1 hour
Total time: about 2 hours
Calories 250, Protein 8g, Cholesterol 55mg, Total fat 10g,
Saturated fat 3g, Sodium 300mg

500 g/1 lb	*fresh beetroots, washed and trimmed, 5 cm (2 inch) stem left on each, or ready-cooked beetroots*
45 g/1¹/₂ oz	*burghul*
1 tbsp	*white vinegar*
1¹/₂ tbsp	*prepared horseradish*
¹/₄ tsp	*salt*
	freshly ground black pepper
175–200 g/ 6-7 oz	*strong plain flour*
1	*egg*
1	*egg white*
1 tbsp	*safflower oil*
Soured cream and chive sauce	
1 tbsp	*virgin olive oil*
1	*small onion, finely chopped*
12.5 cl/4 fl oz	*soured cream*
12.5 cl/4 fl oz	*plain low-fat yogurt*
2 tbsp	*finely cut fresh chives*

If you are using fresh, raw beetroots, preheat the oven to 200°C (400°F or Mark 6). Tightly wrap each beetroot in aluminium foil, with the foil's dull side out. Bake the beetroots until they are tender—about 1 hour. (The beetroots may be cooked up to 24 hours ahead of time.)

Meanwhile, put the burghul in a bowl and pour 12.5 cl (4 fl oz) of boiling water over it. Let the burghul stand for at least 30 minutes.

Peel the beetroots when they are cool enough to handle. Finely chop half of the beetroots and add them to the burghul. Stir in the vinegar, ¹/₂ tablespoon of the horseradish, ¹/₈ teaspoon of the salt and a generous grinding of pepper. Set the mixture aside.

Cut a 2.5 cm (1 inch) thick slice from one of the remaining beetroots and purée it in a blender or food mill—it will yield about 2 tablespoons of purée. Cut the rest of the beetroots into julienne and set them aside in a warm place.

To prepare the pasta dough in a food processor, put 175 g (6 oz) of the flour, the egg, egg white, oil and beetroot purée in the bowl of the machine and process the mixture for about 30 seconds. If the mixture forms a ball immediately and is wet to the touch, mix in flour by the tablespoon until the dough feels soft but not sticky. If the mixture does not form a ball, try pinching it together with your fingers. If it is still too dry to work with, blend in water by the teaspoon until the dough just forms a ball. If you have a pasta machine, the dough may be immediately kneaded and rolled out *(pages 12-13)*.

To prepare the dough by hand, put 175 g (6 oz) of the flour in a mixing bowl and make a well in the centre. Add the egg, egg white, oil and beetroot purée to the well, and stir them with a fork or wooden spoon, gradually mixing in the flour. Transfer the dough to a lightly floured surface and knead it for a few minutes. The dough should come cleanly away from the surface; if it is too wet, add flour by the tablespoon until the dough is no longer sticky If the dough is too dry and crumbly to work with, add water by the teaspoon until the mixture is pliable. Continue kneading the dough until it is smooth and elastic—about 10 minutes; alternatively, knead the dough with a pasta machine *(pages 12-13)*.

If you are not using a pasta machine, wrap the dough in greaseproof paper or plastic film and let it rest for 15 minutes before rolling it out.

Form the dough into ravioli *(page 18)*, filling the ravioli with the beetroot and burghul mixture.

To make the sauce, heat the oil in a heavy-bottomed saucepan over medium-high heat. Add the onion and cook it until it is translucent—about 4 minutes. Reduce the heat to low. Stir in the soured cream and yogurt and heat them through; do not let the sauce boil or the yogurt will separate. Remove the sauce from the heat, then stir in the chives, the remaining $1/8$ teaspoon of salt and the remaining tablespoon of horseradish; keep the sauce warm.

Add the ravioli to 3 litres (5 pints) of boiling water with $1^1/2$ teaspoons of salt. Start testing the ravioli after 3 minutes and cook them until they are *al dente* Drain the pasta, transfer it to a serving dish, and top it with the sauce. Distribute the julienned beetroot around the ravioli and serve the dish immediately.

Spinach Orecchiette Tossed with Cauliflower

Serves 4
Working (and total) time: about 1 hour and 15 minutes
Calories 315, Protein 10g, Cholesterol 30mg, Total fat 13g, Saturated fat 7g, Sodium 275mg

150 g/5 oz	*frozen spinach, washed, stemmed and blanched in boiling water for 1 minute*
90 g/3 oz	*strong plain flour*
140 g/4$^1/_2$ oz	*fine semolina*
60 g/2 oz	*unsalted butter*
1	*small cauliflower (about 750 g/1$^1/_2$ lb) cored and cut into small florets*
$^1/_4$ tsp	*salt*
1 tsp	*fresh thyme, or $^1/_4$ tsp dried thyme freshly ground black pepper*
2	*garlic cloves, finely chopped*
3 tbsp	*dry breadcrumbs*
1 tsp	*chopped fresh sage, or $^1/_4$ tsp dried sage*

To prepare the pasta dough, squeeze the spinach dry then chop it finely. Put the flour and semolina together in a large mixing bowl Add the spinach, then use you hands to combine it with the flours, rubbing the mixture between your fingertips to mix it evenly. Press the dough into a ball. If the dough is too dry to hold together, add, tablespoon of water and mix again. Add more water a teaspoon at a time, if necessary; the dough should be fairly dry. Knead the dough until it is

Moulding Orecchiette

DIMPLING THE DOUGH. After forming a dough roll and cutting off rounds, flatten the pieces. Place a round in the palm of one hand, and indent the centre by pressing the thumb or forefinger of your other hand into it. Repeat with the other rounds.

smooth and elastic—about 10 minutes. Cut the dough into four pieces, then cover three of the pieces with plastic film or an inverted bowl to keep them from drying out.

To form the orecchiette, roll the remaining piece of dough into the shape of a rope about 1 cm (¹/₂ inch) in diameter. With a sharp knife, slice off rounds about 3 mm (¹/₈ inch) thick. Dip the rounds in flour to coat them lightly and make them easier to work with. Put a round in your palm and indent the centre with a finger of your other hand (left, below), flattening the round to a diameter of about 2.5 cm (1 inch). Repeat the process with the remaining rounds of dough and then with the three reserved pieces.

Add the orecchiette to 3 litres (5 pints) of boiling water with 1¹/₂ teaspoons of salt. Start testing after 20 minutes and cook them until they are *al dente*.

While the pasta is cooking, heat half the butter in a large, heavy frying pan over medium-high heat. When the foam subsides, add the cauliflower florets and saute them for 4 minutes, stirring once. Season the cauliflower with the salt, thyme and some pepper. Reduce the heat to medium and continue cooking the cauliflower until it turns golden-brown all over—6 to 8 minutes more. Transfer the florets to a large, warmed bowl.

Reduce the heat under the pan to low. Add the remaining butter and the garlic, and cook for 15 seconds. Add the breadcrumbs, sage and more pepper; cook the breadcrumbs, stirring frequently, until they are a crisp golden-brown—about 4 minutes.

Drain the pasta, transfer it to the bowl with the cauliflower, and toss well. Scatter the breadcrumbs over the top just before serving the dish.

Tomato Fettuccine with Artichokes and Mint

Serves 4

Working (and total) time: about 40 minutes

Calories 310, Protein 9g, Cholesterol 70mg, Total fat 12g, Saturated fat 2g, Sodium 430mg

Tomato pasta dough
1 *egg*
1 *egg white*
3 tbsp *tomato paste*
1 tbsp *virgin olive oil*
175–200 g/6–7 oz *strong plain flour*

Artichoke and mint sauce
6 *artichokes*
1 *lemon, juice only*
1/2 tsp *salt*
freshly ground black pepper
4 *garlic cloves, finely chopped*
2 tbsp *chopped fresh mint or basil*
2 tbsp *virgin olive oil*

To prepare the dough in a food processor, blend the egg, egg white, tomato paste and oil for 5 seconds. Add 175 g (6 oz) of the flour and process for about 30 seconds. If the mixture forms a ball right away and is wet to the touch, mix in flour by the tablespoon until the dough feels soft but not sticky. If the mixture does not form a ball, press it into a ball with your hands. If it is still too dry to work with, blend in water by the teaspoon until the mixture can be formed into a ball. If you have a pasta machine, the dough may be immediately kneaded and rolled out *(pages 12-13)*.

To prepare the dough by hand, put 175 g (6 oz) of the flour in a mixing bowl and make a well in the centre. Add the egg, egg white, tomato paste and oil to the well and mix them, gradually adding the flour. Transfer the dough to a lightly floured surface and knead it for a few minutes. The dough should come cleanly away from the surface; if it is too wet, add flour by the tablespoon until the dough is no longer sticky. If the dough is too dry and crumbly to work with, add water by the teaspoon until it is pliable. Continue kneading the dough until it is smooth and elastic—about 10 minutes; alternatively, knead it in a pasta machine *(pages 12-13)*.

If you are not using a pasta machine, wrap the dough in greaseproof paper or plastic film and let it rest for 15 minutes before rolling it out.

After the dough is rolled out, cut it into fettuccine *(page 13)*. Set the strips aside.

To prepare the artichokes, pour enough water into a large, non-reactive saucepan to fill it about 2.5 cm (1 inch) deep Add the lemon juice, salt, some pepper and the garlic. Break or cut off the stalk of an artichoke. Snap off and discard the leaves, starting at the base and continuing until you reach the pale yellow leaves of the core. Using a large, sharp knife, cut through the base of the pale yellow leaves, then discard them. With a paring knife, trim away any purple leaves and the fuzzy choke, then cut the artichoke bottom into quarters. Cut each quarter into four wedges and drop them

into the water in the pan. Repeat with the remaining five artichokes.

Place the pan over medium-high heat and bring the liquid to the boil. Reduce the heat and simmer the liquid until only 4 tablespoons remain and the artichokes are tender—about 15 minutes.

Meanwhile, bring 3 litres (5 pints) of water to the boil with 1 1/2 teaspoons of salt. Add the fettuccine to the boiling water. Start testing after 2 minutes and cook the pasta until it is *al dente*. Drain the fettuccine and add it to the pan with the artichokes Add the mint or basil and the olive oil, toss well, and serve.

Spinach Pasta Dough
Serves 4

Calories 225, Protein 10g, Cholesterol 60mg, Total fat 7g, Saturated fat 1g, Sodium 120mg

175–200 g/6–7 oz *strong plain flour*
3 tbsp *finely chopped spinach (about 150 g/ 5 oz frozen spinach, thawed, or 250 g/8 oz fresh spinach, washed, stemmed and blanched in boiling water for 1 minute)*
1 *egg*
1 *egg white*
1 tbsp *safflower oil*

To prepare the dough in a food processor, purée the spinach with the egg, egg white and oil for 5 seconds. Add 175 g (6 oz) of the flour and process the mixture for about 30 seconds. If the mixture forms a ball right away and is wet to the touch, mix in flour by the tablespoon until the dough feels soft but not sticky. If the mixture does not form a ball, try pinching it together with your fingers. If it is still too dry to work with, blend in water by the teaspoon until it can be formed into a ball. If you have a pasta machine, the dough may be immediately kneaded and rolled out *(pages 12-13)*.

To prepare the dough by hand, put 175 g (6 oz) of the flour in a mixing bowl and make a well in the centre. Add the spinach, egg, egg white and oil to the well and mix them, gradually incorporating the flour. Transfer the dough to a lightly floured surface and knead it for a few minutes. The dough should come cleanly away from the surface; if it is too wet, add flour by the tablespoon until the dough is no longer sticky. If the dough is too dry and crumbly to work with, add water by the teaspoon until it is pliable. Continue kneading the dough until it is smooth and elastic— about 10 minutes; alternatively, knead the dough in a pasta machine *(pages 12-13)*.

If you are not using a pasta machine, wrap the dough in greaseproof paper or plastic film and let it rest for 15 minutes before rolling it out.

Crab Pillows

Serves 4

Working (and total) time: about 1 hour and 15 minutes

Calories 350, Protein 24g, Cholesterol 145mg, Total fat 10g, Saturated fat 3g, Sodium 325mg

	spinach pasta dough (page 29)
350 g/12 oz	crab meat, all bits of shell removed
6	spring onions, green and white parts separated and thinly sliced
1¹/₂ tsp	finely chopped fresh ginger root
10	drops Tabasco sauce
750 g/1¹/₂ lb	ripe tomatoes, skinned and seeded, or 400 g (14 oz) canned whole tomatoes, drained
1 tbsp	white wine vinegar
1	garlic clove, finely chopped
¹/₈ tsp	cayenne pepper
2 tbsp	double cream

To make the filling, combine the crab meat, the green spring onion parts, the ginger and the Tabasco sauce. Refrigerate the mixture.

To prepare the sauce, first purée the tomatoes in a food processor or blender. Put the purée in a saucepan. Add the vinegar, finely chopped garlic, cayenne pepper and the white spring onion parts, and bring the liquid to the boil. Reduce the heat to low and simmer the tomato sauce for 10 minutes. Set the pan aside.

Divide the pasta dough into two pieces. Roll out each piece into a strip approximately 1 mm (¹/₁₆ inch) thick and 10 cm (4 inches) wide and place the strips on a lightly floured surface *(page 13)*. Cut the strips into 12.5 cm (5 inch) lengths to form 10 by 12.5 cm (4 by 5 inch) rectangles. Spread about 2 tablespoons of the crab filling on one half of each rectangle, leaving an uncovered border about 1 cm (¹/₂ inch) wide. Moisten the edges of the rectangles lightly with your fingers, then fold the dough over the filling to form smaller rectangles that are about 6 by 10 cm (2¹/₂ by 4 inches). Press the edges firmly to seal in the filling. With a fluted pastry wheel or a knife, trim the edges. Use the dull side of a knife to press down along each of the three sealed edges; this leaves a decorative indentation and reinforces the seal.

Cook the pillows in 4 litres (7 pints) of boiling water with 2 teaspoons of salt for 5 minutes, gently turning the pillows over with a slotted spoon half way through the cooking. While the pillows are cooking, warm the sauce over low heat, then whisk in the cream. Spoon half the sauce on to a heated platter.

Remove the pillows from the boiling water with a slotted spoon, allowing most of the water to drain off. Arrange the pillows on the platter. Serve the remaining sauce separately.

Spinach Fettuccine with Chicory and Bacon

Serves 6 as an appetizer
Working (and total) time: about 30 minutes

Calories 215, Protein 8g, Cholesterol 50mg, Total fat 10g,
Saturated fat 2g, Sodium 265mg

	spinach pasta dough (page 29)
5	rashers lean bacon, cut into 1 cm ($\frac{1}{2}$ inch) pieces
1$\frac{1}{2}$ tbsp	virgin olive oil
2	large heads chicory (about 325 g/11 oz), ends trimmed, leaves cut diagonally into 2. 5 cm (1 inch) strips and tossed with 1 tbsp fresh lemon juice
1$\frac{1}{8}$ tsp	salt
	freshly ground black pepper

Roll out the spinach pasta dough and cut it into fettuc-cine *(pages 12-13)*. Set the fettuccine aside on a lightly floured surface.

Meanwhile, cook the bacon pieces in a large, heavy frying pan over medium heat, stirring occasionally, until they are crisp—about 8 minutes. Remove the pan from the heat; with a slotted spoon, transfer the bacon pieces to a paper towel to drain. Pour off all but about 2 tablespoons of the bacon fat from the pan, and re-turn the pan to the heat. Add the olive oil and the chicory. Saute the chicory, stirring frequently, for 2 minutes, then sprinkle it with the salt and some pep-per.

While the chicory cooks, add the fettuccine to 3 li-tres (5 pints) of boiling water with 1$\frac{1}{2}$ teaspoons of salt and cook it until it is *al dente*—about 2 minutes. Drain the pasta and add it to the chicory in the pan. Add the bacon pieces, toss well, and serve at once.

Agnolotti Filled with Turkey Mole

Serves 4 (about 36 agnolotti)
Working (and total) time: about 1 hour
Calories 445, Protein 34g, Cholesterol 140mg, Total Fat
14g, Saturated fat 4g, Sodium 370mg

Turkey Filling

750 g/1¹/₂ lb	whole turkey leg, thigh skinned and boned to yield 140 g (4¹/₂ oz) of meat, the drumstick, bone and remaining meat reserved for the sauce
1 tbsp	safflower oil
2	garlic cloves, finely chopped
1	onion, finely chopped
1	fresh hot green chilli pepper, seeded and finely chopped
¹/₄ tsp	salt
2 tbsp	chopped fresh coriander
1 tbsp	grated plain chocolate

Cocoa pasta dough

175–200 g	strong plain flour
6–7 oz	
1¹/₂ tbsp	cocoa
1	egg
1	egg white

Coriander sauce

2	ripe tomatoes, skinned, seeded and chopped
1	garlic clove, finely chopped
1 tbsp	fresh lemon juice
	freshly ground black pepper
30 g/1 oz	fresh coriander leaves
1	spring onion, thinly sliced

Reserve the weighed turkey thigh meat. Cut the meat from the drumstick, and put it into a saucepan together with the bones and any remaining thigh meat; pour in enough water to cover them by 2.5 cm (1 inch). Cook over medium-high heat until the stock is reduced to 15 cl (¹/₄ pint)—30 to 45 minutes.

Meanwhile, prepare the filling. Mince the reserved turkey meat. Pour the oil into a large, heavy frying pan over low heat. Add the garlic, onion and chilli pepper. Cook, stirring frequently, for 5 minutes. Add the chopped turkey meat and salt, and stir the mixture until it is well blended and the turkey's colour has begun to lighten—about 1 minute. Immediately transfer the filling to a bowl and stir in the coriander and grated chocolate. Refrigerate the filling.

To make the cocoa pasta dough in a food processor, put 175 g (6 oz) of the flour, the cocoa, egg and egg white into the bowl and process for 30 seconds. If the mixture forms a ball immediately and is wet to the touch, mix in flour by the tablespoon until the dough feels soft but not sticky. If the mixture does not form a

ball, try pinching it together with your fingers. If it is still too dry to work with, blend in water by the teaspoon until the dough just forms a ball. If you have a pasta machine, the dough may be immediately kneaded and rolled out *(page 12-13)*.

To prepare the dough by hand, mix the flour and cocoa in a bowl and make a well in the centre. Add the egg and egg white, and stir them with a fork or a wooden spoon, gradually mixing in the flour. Transfer the dough to a lightly floured surface and knead it for a few minutes. The dough should come cleanly away from the surface; if it is too wet, add flour by the tablespoon until the dough is no longer sticky. If the dough is too dry and crumbly to work with, add water by the teaspoon until it is pliable. Continue kneading the dough until it is smooth and elastic—about 10 minutes; alternatively, knead the dough in a pasta machine *(pages 12-13)*.

If you are not using a pasta machine, wrap the dough in greaseproof paper or plastic film and let it rest for 15 minutes before rolling it out.

Divide the dough into three pieces; set two of the pieces aside, covered with plastic film or an inverted bowl. Roll out the remaining piece into a sheet about 1 mm (¹/₁₆ inch) thick. Using a 7.5 cm (3 inch) pastry cutter, cut the sheet into about 12 circles. Place 1 teaspoon of the filling slightly off centre on each circle. Moisten the edges of the circles with water, then fold each circle in half, pressing firmly on the edges to seal in the filling. Repeat with the remaining two pieces of dough to make about 36 agnolotti.

To make the sauce, strain the reduced stock into a saucepan. Add the tomatoes, garlic, lemon juice and some pepper, and bring the liquid to the boil. Reduce the heat to low and simmer the mixture for 3 minutes. Remove the pan from the heat and stir in the coriander and spring onion.

Cook the agnolotti in 3 litres (5 pints) of boiling water with 1¹/₂ teaspoons of salt, stirring once, until the agnolotti float to the top—about 3 minutes. (If necessary to avoid overcrowding, cook the pasta in several batches.) With a slotted spoon, remove the agnolotti and keep them warm. Spoon the sauce over them just before serving.

American Cornmeal Pasta with Chillies and Tomato

Serves 4

Working (and total) time: about 1 hour

Calories 295, Protein 8g, Cholesterol 75mg, Total fat 12g, Saturated fat 3g, Sodium 265mg

Cornmeal pasta dough

90 g/3 oz *finely ground cornmeal*
90 g/3 oz *strong plain flour*
1 *egg white*
1 tbsp *virgin olive oil*

Hot chilli and tomato sauce

1 tbsp *safflower oil*
5 *garlic cloves, peeled and thinly sliced*
2 *small dried red chilli peppers, finely chopped or $^1/_2$ tsp crushed red pepper flakes*
1 *sweet green pepper, seeded, deribbed and chopped*
$^1/_4$ tsp *salt*
1 *large ripe tomato, skinned, seeded and finely chopped*
15 g/$^1/_2$ oz *unsalted butter*

To make the pasta dough, mix the cornmeal and flour in a large bowl. In a small bowl, whisk together the egg, egg white and 3 tablespoons of water. Make a well in the centre of the cornmeal mixture and pour the whisked eggs into the well. Stir the eggs, gradually incorporating the cornmeal mixture into them. When almost all of the dry ingredients are incorpo-

rated, add the olive oil and work it into the dough by hand.

Transfer the dough to a flour-dusted work surface and begin kneading it. If the dough is stiff and crumbly, add water, a teaspoon at a time; if it is too wet and sticky gradually add flour, a tablespoon at a time, until the dough pulls away cleanly from the work surface and no longer sticks to your hands. Knead the dough until it soft and pliable—10 to 15 minutes. Wrap the dough in plastic film to keep it from drying out, then let it rest for 15 minutes to make it easier to roll out.

Dust the work surface with cornmeal. Remove the plastic film and roll the dough into a 60 by 23 cm (29 by 9 inch) rectangle; cut it crosswise into 1 cm ($^1/_2$ inch wide strips.

To prepare the sauce, heat the safflower oil in large, heavy frying pan over medium heat. Add the garlic and red chilli peppers or crushed red pepper flakes, and cook them, stirring frequently, until the garlic turns a light brown—about 4 minutes. Add the sweet green pepper and salt, and cook for 5 minutes more. Stir in the tomato, vinegar and butter, and cook the mixture for an additional 2 minutes.

Add the dough strips to 3 litres (5 pints) of boiling water with 1$^1/_2$ teaspoons of salt; cover the pan. When the water returns to the boil, cook the pasta for 6 minutes. Drain the noodles and add them to the pan containing the sauce. Toss well and serve hot.

Buckwheat Pasta in a Sauce of Green Peppercorns and Mustard

Serves 4

Working (and total) time: about 30 minutes

Calories 375, Protein 13g, Cholesterol 75mg, Total fat 11g, Saturated fat 2g, Sodium 385mg

Buckwheat pasta dough

175 g/6 oz *strong plain flour*
50 g/1$^3/_4$ oz *buckwheat flour*
1 *egg*
1 *egg white*
1 tbsp *safflower oil*

Mustard-peppercorn sauce

1 tbsp *safflower oil*
1 tbsp *finely chopped shallots*
12.5 cl/4 fl oz *dry white wine*
2 tsp *Dijon mustard*
1 tbsp *green peppercorns, crushed*
35 cl/12 fl oz *semi-skimmed milk*
1 *tomato, skinned, seeded and coarsely chopped*
$^1/_2$ tsp *salt*
parsley sprigs for garnish

To prepare the dough in a food processor, put the flours, egg, egg white and oil into the bowl of the machine and process the mixture for about 30 seconds. If the mixture forms a ball immediately and is wet to the touch, mix in flour by the tablespoon until the dough feels soft but not sticky. If the mixture does not form a ball, try pinching it together with your fingers. If it is still too dry to work with, blend in water by the teaspoon until it just forms a ball. Transfer the dough to a floured surface and knead it for a few minutes. If you have a pasta machine, use it to complete the kneading and roll out the dough *(pages 12-13)*.

To prepare the dough by hand, put the flours into a mixing bowl and make a well in the centre. Add the egg, egg white and oil to the well and stir them with a fork or wooden spoon, gradually mixing in the flour. Transfer the dough to a lightly floured surface and knead it for a few minutes. The dough should come cleanly away from the surface; if it is too wet, add flour by the tablespoon until the dough is no longer sticky. If the dough is too dry and crumbly to work with, add water by the teaspoon until it is pliable. Continue kneading the dough until it is smooth and elastic— about 10 minutes; alternatively, knead by hand for a few minutes, then in a pasta machine *(pages 12-13)*.

If you are not using a pasta machine, wrap the dough in greaseproof paper or plastic film and let it rest for 15 minutes before rolling it out. After the dough is rolled out, cut it into fettuccine *(page 13)*.

To prepare the sauce, first heat the oil in a large, heavy-bottomed saucepan over medium-high heat. Add the shallots and saute them until they are translucent—about 1 minute. Add the white wine, mustard and peppercorns. Cook, stirring, until almost all the wine has evaporated. Add the milk, return the mixture to a simmer, and reduce the heat to medium low. Add the noodles and simmer them in the sauce until they are *al dente*—about 3 minutes. Stir in the chopped tomato and season the dish with the salt. Garnish with the parsley and serve immediately.

Pappardelle with Turkey Braised in Red Wine

Serves 8

Working time: about 1 hour and 45 minutes

Total time: about 4 hours

Calories 420, Protein 25g, Cholesterol 90mg, Total fat 10g, Saturated fat 3g, Sodium 240mg

Carrot pasta dough

250 g/8 oz	carrots, peeled and thinly sliced
200 g to 225 g	strong plain flour
7 to 8 oz	
1	egg
1	egg white
1 tbsp	safflower oil

Turkey sauce

1/4 tsp	fresh thyme, or 1/8 tsp dried thyme
1	bay leaf
6	black peppercorns
1	clove
6	juniper berries, or 2 tbsp gin
1	onion, thinly sliced
1	carrot, peeled and thinly sliced
1	stick celery, trimmed and thinly sliced
3	garlic cloves, crushed
3/4 litres/1 1/4 pints	red wine, more if needed
4 tbsp	brandy
3	turkey drumsticks (about 350 g/12 oz each)
4 tbsp	plain flour
1 tbsp	safflower oil
175 g/6 oz	mushrooms, wiped clean, quartered
250 g/8 oz	pearl onions, peeled (optional)
4 tbsp	freshly grated Parmesan cheese

To make the turkey sauce, first prepare a turkey marinade: wrap the thyme, bay leaf, peppercorns, clove and juniper berries, if you are using them, in a 10 cm (4 inch) square piece of muslin. In a large, non-reactive fireproof casserole, combine the gin (if you are using it in place of the juniper berries), the onion, carrot, celery, garlic, the bundle of seasonings and the wine. Bring the mixture to the boil, then lower the heat a simmer it for 15 minutes. Set the casserole aside; when the marinade is cool, stir in the brandy. Put the drum sticks in the casserole. (There should be enough liquid to nearly cover the legs; if there is not, pour in more wine.) Allow the drumsticks to marinate in the refrigerator for at least 2 hours.

For the pasta dough, put the carrots in a saucepan over medium-high heat and pour in enough water cover them. Bring the water to the boil and cook the carrots until they are tender—about 7 minutes. Drain the carrots well and purée them, using a food processor, food mill or sieve. Return the purée to the saucepan and cook over medium heat, stirring constantly, to evaporate as much liquid as possible from the purée without scorching it—about 3 minutes. Set the purée aside.

If you are using a food processor to make the pasta dough, put 200 g (7 oz) of the flour, the egg, egg white, carrot purée and oil in the bowl of the machine and process the mixture for about 30 seconds. If the mixture forms a ball immediately and is wet to the touch, mix in flour by the tablespoon until the dough feels soft but not sticky. If the mixture does not form a ball, try pinching it together with your fingers. If it is still too dry to work with, blend in water by the teaspoon until the dough just forms a ball. If you have a pasta machine, the dough may be immediately kneaded and rolled out (pages 12-13).

To prepare the pasta dough by hand, put 200 g (7 oz) of the flour into a mixing bowl and make a well in the centre. Add the egg, egg white, carrot purée and oil to the well; stir them with a fork or wooden spoon, gradually mixing in the flour. Transfer the dough to a lightly floured surface and knead it for a few minutes. The dough should come cleanly away from the surface; if it is too wet, add flour by the tablespoon until the dough is no longer sticky. If the dough is too dry and crumbly to work with, add water by the teaspoon until it is pliable. Continue kneading the dough until it is smooth and elastic—about 10 minutes, alternatively, knead and roll out the dough in a pasta machine (pages 12-13).

If you are not using a pasta machine, wrap the dough in greaseproof paper or plastic film and let it rest for 15 minutes before rolling it out.

Cut the sheet of dough into pappardelle, using a fluted pastry wheel or a knife to form strips 1 to 2 cm (1/2 to 3/4 inch) wide. (Alternatively, cut the dough into wide fettuccine.) Set the pappardelle aside.

At the end of the turkey-marinating time, preheat the grill. Remove the drumsticks from the casserole, pat the drumsticks dry with paper towels and lightly dredge them in the flour. Brush the drumsticks with the oil and grill them about 7.5 cm (3 inches) below the heat source, turning them to brown, for about 15 minutes. Preheat the oven to 190°C (375°F or Mark 5). Return the drumsticks to the marinade in the casserole, then place the casserole over medium-high heat and bring the marinade to the boil. Cover the casserole tightly and put it in the oven. Braise the turkey until it is tender, turning the drumsticks from time to time so that they cook evenly—about 1 hour.

About 15 minutes before the end of the braising period, put the mushrooms and the pearl onions, if using, in separate saucepans over medium-high heat

and cover the vegetables with water. Bring the water to the boil and cook them until they are tender—about 3 minutes for the mushrooms, 10 minutes for the onions. Drain both pans and set them aside.

Lift the drumsticks from their sauce and put them on a plate. When they are cool enough to handle, remove the skin and discard it. Shred the turkey meat with your fingers, discarding the tendons and sinews, and set the meat aside. Remove the bundle of seasonings from the sauce and discard it. With a slotted spoon, remove the vegetables and purée them.

Skim as much fat as you can from the sauce, then combine the vegetable purée with the sauce. Stir in the turkey meat, mushrooms and, if using, the pearl onions; keep warm while you cook the pasta.

Add the pappardelle to 4 litres (7 pints) of boiling water with 2 teaspoons of salt. Start testing the pappardelle after 1 minute and cook them until they are al dente. Drain the pappardelle and mound them on a large heated serving dish. Pour the sauce over the pasta and serve it immediately. Pass the cheese separately.

Grated Pasta with Green Beans and Cheddar

Serves 6

Working time: about 20 minutes

Total time: about 1 hour and 20 minutes

Calories 230, Protein 12g, Cholesterol 60mg, Total fat 6g, Saturated fat 4g, Sodium 340mg

200 g/7 oz	*strong plain flour*
1	*egg*
1	*egg white*
1/2 tsp	*salt*
125 g/4 oz	*green beans, stemmed, thinly sliced on the diagonal*
1/2 litre/16 fl oz	*skimmed milk*
1/4 tsp	*white pepper*
1/8 tsp	*cayenne pepper*
90 g/3 oz	*grated Cheddar cheese*
4 tbsp	*fresh breadcrumbs*

Put the flour in a mixing bowl and form a well in the middle of the flour. Briefly beat the egg, egg white and 1/4 teaspoon of the salt in another bowl, then pour the beaten egg into the flour. Mix with a large spoon until the flour begins to form clumps. Add enough cold water (1 to 2 tablespoons) to allow you to form the mixture into a ball with your hands. Work the last of the flour into the dough by hand, then turn the dough out on to a flour-dusted surface and knead it until it is firm and smooth—about 5 minutes. Wrap the dough in plastic film and place it in the freezer for at least 1 1/2 hours to harden it.

Remove the dough, unwrap it and grate it on the coarse side of a hand grater. Blanch the beans in boil-ing water for 2 minutes, then refresh them under cold running water. Preheat the oven to 180°C (350°F or Mark 4).

Bring the milk to a simmer over low heat in a large saucepan. Add the grated noodles, white pepper, cayenne pepper and the remaining 1/4 teaspoon of salt. Simmer the mixture, stirring occasionally, until the noodles have absorbed almost all of the liquid—4 to 5 minutes. Add the green beans and half of the grated cheese, and stir thoroughly.

Transfer the contents of the saucepan to an ovenproof casserole. Combine the remaining cheese with the breadcrumbs and sprinkle the mixture over the top. Bake until the crust is crisp and golden—about 20 minutes—and serve hot.

Sweet Potato Gnocchi

Serves 4

Working time: about 35 minutes

Total time: about 1 hour and 35 minutes

Calories 265, Protein 10g, Cholesterol 10mg, Total fat 3g, Saturated fat 1g, Sodium 495mg

500 g/1 lb	*sweet potatoes, baked 1 hour at 200°C (400°F or Mark 6), cooled and peeled*
4 tbsp	*plain low-fat yoghurt*
4 tbsp	*freshly grated Parmesan cheese*
7–8 tbsp	*strong plain flour*
1/4 tsp	*salt*
1/4 tsp	*white pepper*
1/4 tsp	*grated nutmeg*
1/4 tsp	*ground cumin*
3	*egg whites*
1/4 litre/8 fl oz	*unsalted vegetable or chicken stock*
30 g/1 oz	*lean ham, julienned*
2 tbsp	*basil leaves, cut into strips*

Mash the sweet potatoes in a bowl. Add the yoghurt, parmesan cheese and flour, and mix thoroughly with a fork or a wooden spoon (alternatively, put the ingredients in a blender or food processor and mix for 30 seconds, scraping the sides once). Season the mixture with the salt, pepper, nutmeg and cumin, then beat in the egg whites.

Bring 3 litres (5 pints) of water to the boil with 1 1/2 teaspoons of salt. With two tablespoons, form the batter into oval shapes, following the instructions on the opposite page. Drop the gnocchi directly from a spoon into the boiling water, until the pot contains six or seven. When all of the gnocchi return to the surface of the water, start timing; after 3 minutes, transfer the gnocchi with a slotted spoon to a lightly oiled casserole and keep them warm. Repeat this process to cook the remaining batter.

Heat the stock and pour it over the gnocchi. Scatter the ham and basil on top. Serve at once.

Shaping Sweet Potato Gnocchi

1 FILLING THE SPOON. Dip a table-spoon into the batter and heap a little less than a spoonful of the batter on to it. With your other hand take a second tablespoon of the same size and insert it behind the filling at a slight angle.

2 FORMING THE GNOCCHI. Rotate the first spoon backwards and quickly scoop the batter into the second spoon with a flick of the wrist. Scoop the batter back and forth between spoons until the gnocchi has three flattened sides.

3 POACHING THE GNOCCHI. After shaping the gnocchi, dip the spoon into a pot of simmering water and stir gently The gnocchi should come free of the spoon in seconds. Shape the rest of the gnocchi the same way, cooking six or so at a time.

Spinach Gnocchi

Serves 4

Working time: about 40 minutes

Total time: about 1 hour

Calories 265, Protein 18g, Cholesterol 35mg, Total fat 14g, Saturated fat 6g, Sodium 500mg

1	*medium onion, finely chopped*
1 tbsp	*virgin olive oil*
30 g/1 oz	*lean ham, chopped*
300 g/10 oz	*frozen spinach, thawed, or 500 g (1 lb) fresh spinach, washed, stemmed, blanched in boiling water for 1 minute and drained*
125 g/4 oz	*low-fat ricotta cheese*
75 g/2¹/₂ oz	*low-fat cottage cheese*
6 tbsp	*freshly grated Parmesan cheese*
2	*egg whites*
¹/₈ tsp	*grated nutmeg*
60 g/2 oz	*strong plain flour*
15 g/¹/₂ oz	*unsalted butter*

In a small frying pan over medium-high heat, sauté the onion in the oil until the onion is translucent—about 2 minutes. Add the ham and saute for 2 minutes more, then transfer the contents of the pan to a mixing bowl. Use your hands to squeeze the spinach dry. Then chop it finely and put it in the bowl with the onion and ham.

Work the ricotta and cottage cheese through a sieve into the bowl; add 4 tablespoons of the Parmesan cheese, the egg whites, nutmeg and flour. Stir the mixture well and put it into a piping bag fitted with a 1 cm (¹/₂ inch) plain nozzle. Preheat the oven to 200°C (400°F or Mark 6).

In a large pan, bring 4 litres (7 pints) of water to the boil with 2 teaspoons of salt. Meanwhile, pipe 2.5 cm (1 inch) strips of the gnocchi mixture on to large sheets of greaseproof paper, putting about 20 gnocchi in the centre of each sheet. Pick up one of the greaseproof sheets by its edges and dip the gnocchi and paper together into the boiling water; the gnocchi will immediately separate from the paper. Discard the paper. Cook the gnocchi until they rise to the surface of the water and stay there—about 2 minutes. With a slotted spoon, transfer them to a baking dish. Cook the remaining batches of gnocchi the same way.

Dust the gnocchi with the remaining 2 tablespoons of Parmesan cheese and dot them with the butter. Bake the gnocchi until they are sizzling—about 20 minutes—and serve them immediately.

Curry Fettuccine with Chicken and Avocado

Serves 6

Working time: about 45 minutes

Total time: about 2 hours and 15 minutes

Calories 360, Protein 25g, Cholesterol 95mg, Total fat 14g, Saturated fat 2g, Sodium 480mg

	basic pasta dough (page 15), with 1½ tsp curry powder added to the flour
¼ litre/8 fl oz	plain low-fat yoghurt
¾ tsp	curry powder
¾ tsp	salt
1	garlic clove, crushed
5 tbsp	fresh lemon juice
500 g/1 lb	chicken breasts, skinned and boned
½	avocado, peeled and cut into 1 cm (½ inch) cubes
350 g/12 oz	carrots, peeled and sliced into 1 cm (½ inch) rounds
	freshly ground black pepper
2 tbsp	safflower oil
2 tbsp	finely chopped parsley, preferably flat-leaf

In a large, shallow bowl, combine half the yoghurt, ½ teaspoon of the curry powder, ¼ teaspoon of the salt, the garlic and 3 tablespoons of the lemon juice. Arrange the chicken pieces in the bowl in a single layer and spoon the yoghurt mixture over them. Let the chicken marinate in the refrigerator for at least 2 hours, turning it every 30 minutes.

Put the avocado cubes in a small bowl. Pour the remaining 2 tablespoons of lemon juice over them, then toss the cubes gently to coat them. Set aside.

Roll out the pasta dough and cut it into fettuccine (pages 12-13). Set the fettuccine aside.

Put the carrots and the remaining ½ teaspoon of salt in a saucepan. Pour in just enough water to cover the carrots, then bring the water to the boil. Reduce the heat to low, cover the pan, and simmer the carrots until they are tender—15 to 20 minutes. Drain the carrots, reserving 4 tablespoons of their cooking liquid.

In a food mill or food processor, purée the carrots with their reserved cooking liquid. Add the remaining yogurt and curry powder, and purée again. Transfer the mixture to a small saucepan and warm it over low heat. Do not let the sauce boil or the yoghurt will separate.

Meanwhile, wipe the marinade from the chicken breasts and discard it. Sprinkle the chicken with some pepper. Heat the oil in a heavy frying pan over medium-high heat. Add the chicken breasts to the pan and sauté them until they are cooked through—4 to 5 minutes on each side. Cut the meat into chunks; cover the chunks and set them aside in a warm place.

Add the fettuccine to 3 litres (5 pints) of boiling water with 1½ teaspoons of salt. Start testing the fettuccine after 1 minute and cook it until it is al dente.

To assemble the dish, ladle enough of the carrot purée into a heated serving dish to cover the bottom. Arrange the fettuccine on top of the purée. Spoon the remaining purée in a ring around the centre, then mound the chicken in the centre. Scatter the avocado cubes and finely chopped parsley over the chicken, and serve the dish immediately.

Dried Pasta—The Most Varied of Foods

Dried pasta speaks Italian. Any list of available types is almost operatic in the musical sound of its names—from the familiar spaghetti, linguine and lasagne to the more exotic radiatori, bucatini and fusilli. With well over a hundred shapes to tempt the cook and numberless sauces to accompany them, dried pasta ranks among the most varied of foods.

In pasta, as so often in architecture, form can follow function. All these shapes are not just intended to please the eye; many have good reason for their existence. Understanding why they look the way they do can make you a better pasta cook. Consider the spaghetti family. In addition to the familiar pasta most of us have always eaten, it includes capelli d'angelo (angel hair) and vermicelli; among its many cousins are linguine and fettuccine. Although they all share a common trait—ruler-straight lengths— they are not all to be sauced alike. The delicate capelli d'angelo and vermicelli cry out for light treatment—perhaps something as simple as chopped tomatoes, herbs and a little olive oil. The sturdier linguine and fettuccine will hold their own against a thick, strongly flavoured sauce.

Tubular pastas demand a sauce that will cling to them inside and out. Shells and dimpled shapes are exactly right for holding puddles of sauce and bits of meat or fish. Twists allow a luscious sauce to wrap itself around them, yet they will accept a light vinaigrette when served cold as a salad.

Sauce's variety is limited only by the cook's imagination. This section alone includes 53 different kinds, all of them original—from one made with Stilton cheese and port to others of spring greens and lobster, and mushrooms, yoghurt and poppy seeds. At the same time as it offers such audacious combinations as these, the section takes some fresh approaches to familiar dishes. There is, for example, lasagne prepared with Gorgonzola cheese and Batavian endive. The traditional pasta with basil pesto is the inspiration for a rocket pesto, greener than its prototype yet every bit as delicious. Another dish starts with the fresh ingredients of a basil pesto—basil, pine-nuts and garlic—and instead of reducing them to a thick purée adds them directly to the pasta. The section even includes a couple of pasta dishes cooked right in the sauce. The pasta's starch thickens the sauce, while the sauce flavours the pasta. What could be easier?

43

A Pasta Primer

ditalini
salad macaroni

elbow macaroni

ziti

penne

penne rigati

rigatoni

capelli d'angelo
capellini

vermicelli

thin spaghetti
spaghettini

spaghetti

bucatini
perciatelli

long fusilli
fusilli lunghi

cannelloni

RIBBON

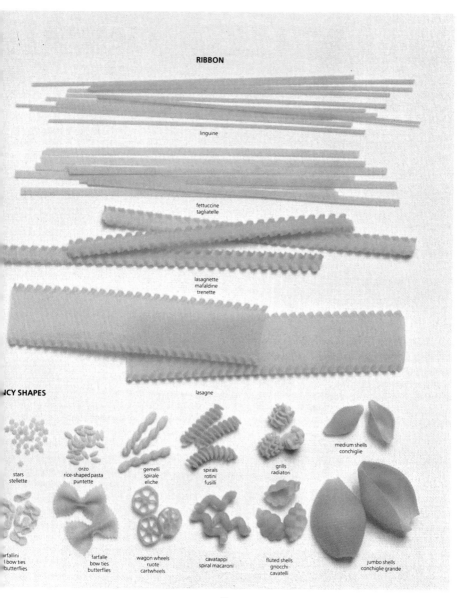

linguine

fettuccine
tagliatelle

lasagnette
mafaldine
trenette

lasagne

NCY SHAPES

stars
stellette

orzo
rice-shaped pasta
puntette

gemelli
spirale
eliche

spirals
rotini
fusilli

grills
radiatori

medium shells
conchiglie

arfallini
l bow ties
butterflies

farfalle
bow ties
butterflies

wagon wheels
ruote
cartwheels

cavatappi
spiral macaroni

fluted shells
gnocchi
cavatelli

jumbo shells
conchiglie grande

45

Linguine with Broad Beans and Grainy Mustard

Serves 4

Working (and total) time: about 20 minutes

Calories 345, Protein 12g, Cholesterol 15mg, Total fat 8g,
Saturated fat 4g, Sodium 325mg

250 g/8 oz	*linguine (or spaghetti)*
250 g/8 oz	*ripe plum tomatoes*
17.5 cl/6 fl oz	*unsalted chicken stock*
165 g/5½ oz	*fresh or frozen young broad beans*
¼ tsp	*salt*
2	*spring onions, trimmed and thinly sliced*
1½ tbsp	*grainy mustard*
30 g/1 oz	*unsalted butter*

Place a tomato on a cutting surface with its stem end down. With a small, sharp knife, cut wide strips of flesh from the tomato, discarding its seeds and juice. Slice each piece of tomato flesh into 5 mm (¼ inch) wide strips and set them aside. Repeat the process with the remaining tomatoes.

Pour the stock into a large, heavy frying pan over medium heat and bring it to a simmer. Add the broad beans and salt, and cook for 6 minutes. Stir in the spring onions and mustard; simmer for 1 minute more. Add the butter and tomato strips, then simmer the mixture for an additional 2 minutes, stirring once.

Meanwhile, cook the linguine in 3 litres (5 pints) of boiling water with 1½ teaspoons of salt. Start testing the pasta after 10 minutes and cook it until it is *al dente*. Drain the linguine and transfer it to the pan with the broad bean mixture. Toss well to coat the pasta and serve immediately.

EDITOR'S NOTE: If plum tomatoes are not available, an equivalent amount of another variety of tomato may be used.

Penne Rigati with Mushrooms and Tarragon

Serves 4

Working (and total) time: about 45 minutes

Calories 385, Protein 11g, Cholesterol 0mg, Total Fat 8g,
Saturated Fat 1g, Sodium 385mg

250 g/8 oz	*penne rigati (or other short, tubular pasta)*
15 g/¹/₂ oz	*dried ceps, or porcini mushrooms*
2 tbsp	*virgin olive oil*
1	*small onion, finely chopped*
250 g/8 oz	*button mushrooms, cut into 5 mm (¹/₄ inch) dice*
¹/₂ tsp	*salt*
	freshly ground black pepper
3	*garlic cloves, finely chopped*
litre/8 fl oz	*dry white wine*
¹50 g/1¹/₂ lb	*tomatoes, skinned, seeded and chopped*
6 tbsp	*chopped parsley*
2 tbsp	*chopped fresh tarragon*

Pour ¹/₄ litre (8 fl oz) of hot water over the dried mushrooms and soak them until they are soft—about 20

minutes. Drain the ceps and reserve their soaking liquid. Cut them into 5 mm (¹/₄ inch) pieces.

Heat the oil in a large, heavy frying pan over medium heat. Add the onion and saute it until it turns
translucent—about 4 minutes. Add the ceps and but-
ton mushrooms, salt and pepper. Cook until the mushrooms begin to brown—about 5 minutes. Add the garlic and the wine, and cook the mixture until the liquid
is reduced to approximately 2 tablespoons—about 5
minutes more.

Add the penne rigati to 3 litres (5 pints) of boiling
water with 1¹/₂ teaspoons of salt. Start testing the pasta
after 10 minutes and continue to cook it until it is *al
dente.*

While the penne rigati is cooking, pour the reserved
cep-soaking liquid into the pan containing the mushrooms and cook until the liquid is reduced to approximately 4 tablespoons—about 5 minutes. Stir in the
tomatoes and cook the mixture until it is heated
through—about 3 minutes more. Drain the pasta and
add it to the pan along with the chopped parsley and
tarragon. Toss well and serve.

Bucatini with Carrot and Courgette Serpents

Serves 6 as an appetizer
Working time: about 20 minutes
Total time: about 30 minutes
Calories 210, Protein 6g, Cholesterol 5mg, Total fat 5g,
Saturated fat 1g, Sodium 70mg

250 g/8 oz *bucatini (or linguine)*
2 *carrots*
3 *medium courgettes, washed, ends removed*
2 tbsp *virgin olive oil*
6 *large garlic cloves, peeled, each sliced into 4 or 5 pieces*
2 *anchovy fillets, finely chopped*
90 g/3 oz *red onion, thinly sliced*
freshly ground black pepper

Fashion the carrot and courgette serpents: pressing down hard on a sharp vegetable peeler, grate along the length of a carrot to detach a wide strip. Continue removing strips until you reach the woody core, then turn the carrot over and repeat the process on the other side. Peel strips from the other carrot in the same manner, then cut each strip lengthwise into 5 mm (" inch) wide serpents. With a small, sharp knife, cut long strip about 2.5 cm (1 inch) wide and 5 mm (" inch) thick from the outside of a courgette. Continu cutting strips to remove the green outer portion of the courgettes. Discard the seedy inner cores. Cut each strip lengthwise into serpents 3 mm (⅛ inch) wide.

Put 3 litres (5 pints) of water on to boil with 1½ teaspoons of salt. Heat the oil in a large, heavy frying pan over low heat. Add the garlic slices and cook them stirring occasionally, until they are golden-brown both sides—10 to 15 minutes. About 5 minutes after adding the garlic to the pan, drop the pasta into the boiling water. Start testing the pasta after 12 minutes and continue to cook it until it is *al dente*.

When the garlic slices have turned golden-brown add the anchovy fillets, onion, carrots and courgettes to the pan; cover the pan, and cook for 3 minutes Remove the cover and cook the mixture, stirring frequently, for 3 minutes more.

Drain the pasta and immediately add it to the pan Add some pepper, toss well, and serve at once.

Fettuccine with Artichokes and Tomatoes

Serves 4

Working time: about 25 minutes

Total time: about 50 minutes

Calories 290, Protein 12g, Cholesterol 5mg, Total fat 3g, Saturated fat 1g, Sodium 345mg

250 g/8 oz	*fettuccine (or other narrow ribbon pasta)*
750 g/1¹/₂ lb	*ripe tomatoes, skinned and chopped, seeds and juice reserved, or 800 g (28 oz) canned whole tomatoes, drained and chopped*
1	*onion, chopped*
1	*carrot, peeled, quartered lengthwise and cut into 5 mm (¹/₄ inch) pieces*
1 tsp	*fresh thyme, or ¹/₄ tsp dried thyme*
1 tsp	*chopped fresh rosemary, or ¹/₄ tsp dried rosemary*
¹/₄ tsp	*salt*
	freshly ground black pepper
3	*fresh artichoke bottoms, rubbed with the juice of 1 lemon*
1 tbsp	*red wine vinegar or cider vinegar*
4 tbsp	*freshly grated Parmesan cheese*

Put the chopped tomatoes, onion, carrot, the thyme and rosemary if you are using fresh herbs, and the salt and pepper in a saucepan over medium-high heat. Bring the mixture to the boil, reduce the heat to low, and simmer the mixture for 5 minutes.

Slice the artichoke bottoms into strips 3 mm (¹/₈ inch) wide and add them to the pan. If you are using dried herbs, add them now. Pour in the vinegar and simmer the mixture, uncovered, for 15 minutes. Add the reserved tomato seeds and juice, if you are using fresh tomatoes, and continue cooking until most of the liquid has evaporated and the artichoke bottoms are tender but not mushy—about 15 minutes more.

Approximately 15 minutes before the vegetables finish cooking, add the fettuccine to 3 litres (5 pints) boiling water with 1¹/₂ teaspoons of salt. Start testing the pasta after 10 minutes and cook it until it is *al dente*. Drain it and add it immediately to the sauce. Sprinkle the cheese over the top, toss lightly and serve.

Sweet-and-Sour Cabbage Cannelloni

Serves 6

Working time: about 45 minutes

Total time: about 1 hour and 30 minutes

Calories 295, Protein 9g, Cholesterol 10mg, Total fat 6g,
Saturated fat 3g, Sodium 190mg

12	*cannelloni (about 250 g/12 oz)*
30 g/1 oz	*unsalted butter*
1	*small onion, finely chopped*
500 g/1 lb	*green cabbage, shredded*
1	*carrot, peeled and grated*
1	*apple, peeled, cored and grated*
1/4 tsp	*salt*
1.25 kg/2 1/2 lb	*ripe tomatoes quartered*
1 tbsp	*dark brown sugar*
2 tbsp	*white wine vinegar*
4 tbsp	*raisins*
1/4 litre/8 fl oz	*unsalted chicken stock*

To prepare the cabbage stuffing, melt the butter in a large, heavy frying pan over medium heat. Add the onion and sauté it until it turns translucent—about 4 minutes. Pour enough water into the pan to fill it 5 mm (1/4 inch) deep. Stir in the cabbage, carrot, apple and 1/8 teaspoon of the salt. Cover the pan and steam the vegetables and apple, adding more water as necessary, until they are soft—about 30 minutes. Set the pan aside.

Meanwhile, pour 4 tablespoons of water into a saucepan over medium-high heat. Add the tomatoes and cook them, stirring frequently, until they are quite soft—about 20 minutes. Transfer the tomatoes to a sieve and allow their clear liquid to drain off. Discard the liquid and purée the tomatoes into a bowl. Stir in the brown sugar, vinegar, raisins and the remaining 1/8 teaspoon of salt.

To prepare the cannelloni, add the tubes to 4 litres (7 pints) of boiling water with 2 teaspoons of salt. Start testing the cannelloni after 15 minutes and cook them until they are al dente. With a slotted spoon, transfer the tubes to a large bowl of cold water.

Preheat the oven to 200°C (400°F or Mark 6). Thoroughly drain the cannelloni and fill each one carefully with about one twelfth of the cabbage stuffing.

Arrange the tubes in a single layer in a large baking dish. Pour the stock over the tubes and cover the dish

tightly with aluminium foil. Bake for 30 minutes. Ten minutes before serving time, transfer the sauce from the bowl to a saucepan and bring it to the boil. Reduce the heat to low and let the sauce simmer gently while the cannelloni finish cooking. Serve the cannelloni immediately; pass the sauce separately.

EDITOR S NOTE: To allow for cannelloni tubes that may tear during cooking or while being stuffed, add one or two extra tubes to the boiling water. The cannelloni may be assembled in advance and refrigerated for up to 24 hours before the stock is added and the dish is baked.

Penne with Squid in Tomato-Fennel Sauce

Serves 4

Working time: about 35 minutes

Total time: about 1 hour

Calories 360, Protein 20g, Cholesterol 120mg, Total Fat 5g, Saturated Fat 1g, Sodium 315mg

250 g/8 oz	*penne (or other short, tubular pasta)*
350 g/12 oz	*squid*
1 tbsp	*safflower oil*
4 tbsp	*anise-flavoured liqueur, or 1 tsp fennel seeds*
750 g/1¹/₂ lb	*tomatoes, skinned, seeded and chopped, or 400 g (14 oz) canned tomatoes, drained and chopped*
1	*fennel bulb, stalks discarded, bulb grated*
6	*spring onions, trimmed and finely chopped*
¹/₄ tsp	*salt*
	freshly ground black pepper

To clean a squid, first gently pull the quill-shaped pen out of its body pouch. Then, holding the body pouch in one hand and the head in the other, pull the two sections apart; the viscera will come away with the head. Rinse the body pouch thoroughly and rub off the thin purplish skin covering it. Remove the triangular fins and skin them too, then slice them into strips. Cut the tentacles from the head, slicing just below the eyes. Cut out the hard beak from the centre of the tentacles and discard it. Slice the body pouch into thin rings. Repeat these steps to clean the rest of the squid.

Heat the oil in a large, heavy frying pan over medium-high heat. Saute the squid in the oil for 1 to 2 minutes. Pour in the liqueur if you are using it, and cook the mixture for 30 seconds more. With a slotted spoon, transfer the squid to a plate. Add the tomatoes, fennel, fennel seeds if you are using them, and the spring onions to the pan. Reduce the heat to low and simmer the mixture, stirring occasionally, until the fennel is soft—20 to 25 minutes.

When the fennel has been simmering for about 10 minutes, add the penne to 3 litres (5 pints) of boiling water with 1¹/₂ teaspoons of salt. Start testing the pasta after 10 minutes and cook it until it is *al dente*.

When the pasta is almost done, return the squid to the sauce and gently heat it through—2 to 3 minutes. Season the sauce with the salt and the pepper. Drain the pasta, transfer it to a bowl and toss it with the sauce. Serve immediately.

Spaghetti with Fresh Basil, Pine-Nuts and Cheese

Serves 4
Working (and total) time: about 15 minutes
Calories 360, Protein 14g, Cholesterol 15mg, Total fat 13g, Saturated fat 3g, Sodium 415mg

250 g/8 oz	*spaghetti*
1 tbsp	*virgin olive oil*
1	*garlic clove, crushed*
60 g/2 oz	*basil leaves, shredded, plus several whole leaves reserved for garnish*
12.5 cl/4 fl oz	*unsalted chicken stock*
30 g/1 oz	*pine-nuts, toasted in a small, dry frying pan over medium heat*
60 g/2 oz	*pecorino cheese, freshly grated*

$^1/_4$ tsp *salt*
freshly ground black pepper

To prepare the sauce, first pour the oil into a frying pan set over medium heat. When the oil is hot, add the garlic and cook it, stirring constantly, for about 30 seconds. Reduce the heat to low. Stir in the shredded basil leaves and allow them to wilt—approximately 30 seconds. Pour in the stock and simmer the liquid gently while you cook the pasta.

Add the spaghetti to 3 litres (5 pints) of boiling water with 1$^1/_2$ teaspoons of salt. Start testing the pasta after 10 minutes and cook it until it is *al dente*.

Drain the pasta and add it to the pan with the basil. Toss well to coat the pasta. Add the pine-nuts, cheese, salt and some pepper, and toss again. Serve at once, garnished with the whole basil leaves.

Gorgonzola Lasagne

Serves 8

Working time: about 45 minutes
Total time: about 1 hour and 30 minutes
Calories 205, Protein 9g, Cholesterol 15mg, Total fat 8g,
Saturated Fat 3g, Sodium 245mg

250 g/8 oz	*lasagne*
4	*sweet red peppers*
350 g/12 oz	*red onions, sliced into 1 cm (¹/₂ inch)*
	rounds
2 tbsp	*fresh lemon juice*
1 tbsp	*fresh thyme, or ¹/₄ tsp dried thyme*
2 tbsp	*virgin olive oil*
500 g/1 lb	*Batavian endive, washed, trimmed and*
	sliced crosswise into 2.5 cm (1 inch) strips
¹/₂ tsp	*salt*
	freshly ground black pepper
4 tbsp	*freshly grated Parmesan cheese*
125 g/4 oz	*Gorgonzola cheese, broken into small*
	pieces

Preheat the grill. Arrange the peppers in the centre of a baking sheet with the onion slices surrounding them.

Grill the vegetables until the peppers are blistered on all sides and the onions are lightly browned—10 to 15 minutes. (You will need to turn the peppers a few times, the onions once.) Put the peppers in a bowl, cover it with plastic film, and set it aside. Separate the onion slices into rings and reserve them as well.

Cook the lasagne in 3 litres (5 pints) of boiling unsalted water with the lemon juice for 7 minutes—the pasta will be slightly underdone. Drain the pasta and run cold water over it.

Peel the peppers when they are cool enough to handle, working over a bowl to catch the juices. Remove the stem, seeds and ribs from each pepper. Set one pepper aside and slice the remaining three into lengthwise strips about 2 cm (³/₄ inch) wide. Strain the pepper juices and reserve them.

Quarter the reserved whole pepper; purée the pieces in a food processor or blender with the pepper juices and 2 teaspoons of the fresh thyme or $1/2$ teaspoon of the dried thyme. Preheat the oven to 180°C (350°F or Mark 4).

Heat the oil in a large, heavy frying pan over medium-high heat. Add the Batavian endive, $1/4$ teaspoon of the salt, the remaining teaspoon of fresh thyme or $1/4$ teaspoon of dried thyme, and a generous grinding of black pepper. Sauté the endive until it is wilted and almost all the liquid has evaporated— about 5 minutes. Remove the pan from the heat.

Line the bottom of a baking dish with a layer of the lasagne. Cover this layer with half of the endive and sprinkle it with 1 tablespoon of the Parmesan cheese. Spread half of the pepper strips over the top, then cover them with half of the onion rings. Build a second layer of lasagne, endive, Parmesan cheese, pepper strips and onion rings, this time topping the onion rings with half of the pepper purée. Cover the second level with a final layer of lasagne, and spread the remaining purée over the top. Scatter the Gorgonzola cheese evenly over the pepper sauce and sprinkle the remaining 2 tablespoons of Parmesan cheese over all.

Bake the lasagne for 30 minutes. Let the dish stand for 10 minutes to allow the flavours to meld.

Pasta Salad with Lobster and Mange-Tout

Serves 4
Working time: about 40 minutes
Total time: about 1 hour
Calories 375, Protein 17g, Cholesterol 40mg, Total fat 12g, Saturated fat 1g, Sodium 270mg

250 g/8 oz	radiatori (or other fancy pasta)
4 tbsp	very thinly sliced shallots
1 tbsp	red wine vinegar
3 tbsp	virgin olive oil
2	garlic cloves, lightly crushed
$1/4$ tsp	salt
	freshly ground black pepper
1	live lobster (about 750 g/$1^1/2$ lb)
2 tbsp	lemon juice
250 g/8 oz	mange-tout, trimmed and strings removed, sliced in half with a diagonal cut
1 tbsp	chopped fresh basil or flat-leaf parsley

Pour enough water into a large pot to fill it about 2.5 cm (1 inch) deep Bring the water to the boil and add the lobster. Cover the pot tightly and steam the lobster until it turns a bright reddish orange—about 12 minutes.

In the meantime, put half of the sliced shallots in a bowl with the vinegar and let them stand for 5 minutes.

Whisk in 2 tablespoons of the oil, then stir in the garlic $1/8$ teaspoon of the salt, and some freshly ground pepper. Set the vinaigrette aside.

Remove the lobster from the pot and set it on a dish to catch the juices. Pour 2 litres (3$1/2$ pints) of water into the pot along with 1 tablespoon of the lemon juice, and bring the liquid to the boil.

When the lobster has cooled enough to handle, twist off the tail and claws from the body. Crack the shell and remove the meat from the tail and claws. Add the shells and the body to the boiling liquid and cook for 10 minutes. Cut the meat into 1 cm ($1/2$ inch) pieces and set it aside in a bowl.

Use a slotted spoon to remove the shells from the boiling liquid; then add the pasta. Start testing after 13 minutes and cook the pasta until it is al dente.

While the pasta is cooking, pour the remaining oil into a large, heavy frying pan over medium-high heat. Add the mange-tout together with the remaining 2 tablespoons of shallots and $1/8$ teaspoon of salt. Cook, stirring constantly, until the mange-tout turn bright green—about 1$1/2$ minutes. Scrape the contents of the pan into the bowl with the lobster.

When the pasta finishes cooking, drain it and rinse it briefly under cold water. Remove and discard the garlic from the vinaigrette, then combine the vinaigrette with the pasta. Add the lobster mixture, the basil, the remaining tablespoon of lemon juice and some more pepper, and toss well.

EDITOR'S NOTE: Although the pasta salad may be served immediately, allowing it to stand for 30 minutes will meld its flavours.
Alternatively, the salad may be served chilled.

Pinto Beans and Wagon Wheels

Serves 4

Working time: about 25 minutes

Total time: about 9 hours and 30 minutes

Calories 575, Protein 32g, Cholesterol 35mg, Total fat
13g, Saturated fat 3g, Sodium 470mg

250 g/8 oz	*wagon wheels (or other fancy-shaped or short, tubular pasta)*
90 g/6¹/₂ oz	*dried pinto or red kidney beans, soaked for 8 hours in water to cover and drained*
2 tbsp	*safflower oil*
175 g/6 oz	*boneless topside of beef, cut into 1 cm (¹/₂ inch) cubes*
1	*small onion, finely chopped*
1	*sweet green pepper, seeded, deribbed and cut into 1 cm (¹/₂ inch) squares*
1	*garlic clove, very finely chopped*
1.25 kg/2¹/₂ lb	*ripe tomatoes, skinned, seeded and chopped, or 800 g (28 oz) canned whole tomatoes, drained and chopped*
5	*drops Tabasco sauce*
1 tbsp	*coarsely chopped fresh coriander*

freshly ground black pepper

¹/₂ tsp *salt*

4 tbsp *grated Cheddar cheese*

Cook the beans in ³/₄ litre (1¹/₄ pints) of boiling water for 10 minutes, then drain them and set them aside.

While the beans are boiling, heat the safflower oil in a large, heavy frying pan over medium-high heat. Brown the beef in the oil, stirring frequently, for 3 minutes. Remove the meat from the pan with a slotted spoon and set it aside.

Cook the onion and green pepper in the oil remaining in the pan until the onion turns translucent— about 3 minutes. Add the garlic and cook for half a minute more, then return the beef to the pan. Stir in the tomatoes, pinto beans and ¹/₄ litre (8 fl oz) of warm water, and bring the mixture to a simmer. Cover the pan, reduce the heat to low and simmer until the beans are tender—about 1 hour and 10 minutes.

Approximately 10 minutes before the pinto beans finish cooking, add the wagon wheels to 3 litres (5 pints) of boiling water with 1¹/₂ teaspoons of salt. Start

testing the pasta after 8 minutes and continue to cook until it is *al dente*.

Drain the wagon wheels and add them to the bean mixture; stir in the Tabasco sauce, coriander, black pepper, and salt. Simmer for 3 minutes more, then transfer the contents of the pan to a serving dish; sprinkle the cheese over the top and serve at once.

EDITOR'S NOTE: As a time-saving alternative to soaking the pinto beans for 8 hours, boil them in 3/4 litre (1 1/4 pints) of water for 2 minutes, then remove the pan from the heat cover it, and let the beans soak for 1 hour. Drain the beans and boil them in fresh water for 10 minutes, as above, before adding them to the frying pan.

Fluted Shells with Spicy Carrot Sauce

Serves 6 as an appetizer or side dish
Working time: about 15 minutes
Total time: about 1 hour
Calories 185, Protein 7g, Cholesterol 40mg, Total fat 4g,
Saturated fat 29, Sodium 200mg

250 g/8 oz	*fluted shells (or other shell-shaped pasta)*
250 g/8 oz	*carrots, peeled and finely chopped*
1	*stick celery, finely chopped*
4	*garlic cloves, finely chopped*
1/4 tsp	*crushed red pepper flakes*
1 tbsp	*fresh thyme, or 1 tsp dried thyme*
1/2 litre/16 fl oz	*unsalted chicken or vegetable stock*
4 tbsp	*red wine vinegar*
15 g/1/2 oz	*unsalted butter*
1/4 tsp	*salt*
	freshly ground black pepper

Put the carrots, celery, garlic, red pepper flakes, thyme and enough water to cover them in a saucepan. Bring the mixture to the boil, then cover the pan and reduce the heat to medium. Simmer the vegetables until they are tender—about 20 minutes.

Pour 1/4 litre (8 fl oz) of the stock into the carrot mixture and cook until the liquid is reduced to approximately 4 tablespoons—about 10 minutes. Add the remaining stock and the vinegar, and cook until only 4 tablespoons of liquid remain—about 10 minutes more.

While you are reducing the second portion of stock, cook the pasta in 3 litres (5 pints) of boiling water with 1 1/2 teaspoons of salt. Start testing the pasta after 5 minutes and cook it until it is *al dente*.

Stir the butter, salt and pepper into the sauce. Drain the pasta, put it in a bowl, and toss it with the sauce.

Chilled Spirals with Rocket Pesto

Serves 4

Working time about 25 minutes

Total time: about 2 hours

Calories 535, Protein 17g, Cholesterol 10mg, Total fat
22g, Saturated fat 4g, Sodium 395mg

350 g/12 oz *spirals*
125 g/4 oz *rocket, washed, cleaned and stemmed*
1 *small garlic clove, coarsely chopped*
30 g/1 oz *pine-nuts*
3 tbsp *virgin olive oil*
1 tbsp *safflower oil*
60 g/2 oz *Parmesan cheese, freshly grated*
1/4 tsp *salt*
freshly ground black pepper
1 *sweet red pepper, seeded, deribbed and
finely diced*
2 tbsp *balsamic vinegar, or 1 tbsp red wine
vinegar*

Add the spirals to 4 litres (7 pints) of boiling water with
2 teaspoons of salt. Start testing the pasta after 8 minutes and cook it until it is *al dente*.

Meanwhile, prepare the pesto: put the rocket, garlic, pine-nuts, olive oil and safflower oil in a blender or
food processor. Blend for 2 minutes, stopping two or
three times to scrape down the sides. Add the cheese
and the salt; blend the mixture briefly to form a purée.

Drain the pasta, transfer it to a large bowl, and season it with some black pepper. Add the diced red pepper, the vinegar and pesto, and toss well. Chill the
pasta salad in the refrigerator for 1 to 2 hours before
serving it.

Ziti with Italian Sausage and Red Peppers

Serves 4

Working time: about 30 minutes

Total time: about 40 minutes

Calories 300, Protein 11g, Cholesterol 10mg, Total Fat 7g, Saturated Fat 2g, Sodium 330mg

250 g/8 oz	*ziti (or other tubular pasta)*
3	*sweet red peppers*
125 g/4 oz	*spicy Italian pork sausages*
2	*garlic cloves, finely chopped*
2 tsp	*fresh thyme, or ¹/₂ tsp dried thyme*
1	*large tomato, skinned, seeded and puréed*
1 tbsp	*red wine vinegar*
¹/₈ tsp	*salt*

Preheat the grill. Place the peppers 5 cm (2 inches) below the heat source, turning them from time to time, until they are blackened all over—15 to 18 minutes. Put the peppers in a bowl and cover it with plastic film. The trapped steam will loosen their skins.

Squeeze the sausages out of their casings and break the meat into small pieces; sauté the pieces over medium-high heat until they are browned—about 3 minutes. Remove the pan from the heat and stir in the garlic and thyme.

Add the pasta to 3 litres (5 pints) of boiling water with 1¹/₂ teaspoons of salt; start testing it after 10 minutes and cook it until it is *al dente*.

While the pasta is cooking, peel the peppers, working over a bowl to catch the juices. Remove and discard the stems, seeds and ribs; strain the juices and reserve them. Slice the peppers lengthwise into thin strips.

Set the pan containing the sausage mixture over medium heat. Add the pepper strips and their reserved juices, the puréed tomato, the vinegar and the ¹/₈ teaspoon of salt. Simmer the sauce until it thickens and is reduced by about one third—5 to 7 minutes.

Drain the pasta, return it to the pan, and combine it with the sauce. Cover the pan and let the pasta stand for 5 minutes to allow the flavours to blend.

Vermicelli, Onions and Peas

Serves 8 as a side dish
Working time: about 15 minutes
Total time: about 1 hour
Calories 185, Protein 5g, Cholesterol 0mg, Total fat 4g,
Saturated fat 1g, Sodium 120mg

250 g/8 oz	*vermicelli or spaghettini*
2 tbsp	*virgin olive oil*
500 g/1 lb	*onions, chopped*
1	*leek, trimmed, cleaned and thinly sliced*
¹/₄ tsp	*salt*
	freshly ground black pepper
¹/₄ litre/8 fl oz	*dry white wine*
75 g/2¹/₂ oz	*shelled peas*

Heat the oil in a large, heavy frying pan over low heat. Add the onions, leek, salt and a generous grinding of pepper. Cover the pan tightly and cook, stirring fre-quently to keep the onions from sticking, until the veg-etables are very soft—about 45 minutes.

Cook the pasta in 3 litres (5 pints) of boiling water with 1¹/₂ teaspoons of salt. Start testing the pasta af-ter 7 minutes and cook it until it is *al dente.*

While the pasta is cooking, finish the sauce: pour the wine into the pan and raise the heat to high. Cook the mixture until the liquid is reduced to about 4 table-spoons—approximately 5 minutes. Stir in the peas, cover the pan, and cook for another 1 to 2 minutes to heat the peas through. If you are using fresh peas, increase the cooking time to 5 minutes.

Drain the pasta and transfer it to a serving dish; pour the contents of the frying pan over the top and toss well. Serve immediately.

Lasagne Roll-Ups

Serves 6

Working time: about 45 minutes

Total time: about 1 hour and 10 minutes

Calories 445, Protein 24g, Cholesterol 35mg, Total fat
16g, Saturated fat 7g, Sodium 340mg

12	*lasagne strips*
500 g/1 lb	*low-fat ricotta cheese*
125 g/4 oz	*low-fat mozzarella, shredded*
250 g/8 oz	*broccoli, steamed for 5 minutes, drained and chopped*
75 g/2½ oz	*mushrooms, sliced*
2	*spring onions, trimmed and chopped*
2 tbsp	*chopped fresh basil, or 2 tsp dried basil*
1 tbsp	*chopped fresh oregano, or 1 tsp dried oregano*
4 tbsp	*chopped parsley*

Tomato sauce

2 tbsp	*safflower oil*
1	*onion, coarsely chopped*
2	*small carrots, peeled and coarsely chopped*
2	*sticks celery, trimmed and coarsely chopped*
2	*garlic cloves, thinly sliced*
3 tbsp	*chopped fresh basil, or 1 tbsp dried basil*
	freshly ground black pepper
1	*bay leaf*
15 cl/¼ pint	*Madeira*
.25 kg/2½ lb	*ripe tomatoes, skinned, seeded and chopped, or 800 g (28 oz) canned whole tomatoes, drained and chopped*
2 tbsp	*tomato paste*
125 g/4 oz	*unsweetened apple purée*
3 tbsp	*freshly grated Parmesan cheese*

To make the sauce, pour the oil into a large, heavy-bottomed saucepan over medium-high heat. Add the onion, carrots and celery. Sauté the mixture, stirring frequently, for 2 minutes. Add the garlic and cook for 1 minute more. Stir in the basil, pepper, bay leaf and Madeira. Bring the liquid to the boil and cook it until it is reduced by about half—2 to 3 minutes. Add the tomatoes, tomato paste and apple purée. As soon as the liquid returns to the boil, reduce the heat to low and gently simmer the sauce for 30 to 35 minutes. Remove the bay leaf and transfer the sauce to a food processor or blender. Purée the sauce and return it to the saucepan. Stir in the grated Parmesan cheese and set the pan aside.

Preheat the oven to 180°C (350°F or Mark 4). Add the lasagne to 4 litres (7 pints) of boiling water with 2 teaspoons of salt. Start testing the pasta after 12 minutes and cook it until it is *al dente*. Drain the pieces

and spread them on a clean tea towel to dry.

In a large bowl, mix the ricotta, mozzarella, broccoli, mushrooms, spring onions, basil, oregano and parsley.

To assemble the dish, spread ¼ litre (8 fl oz) of the tomato sauce over the bottom of a 28 by 33 cm (11 by 13 inch) baking dish. Spread about 4 tablespoons of the cheese and vegetable mixture over a lasagne strip; starting at one end, roll up the strip. Place the roll, seam side down, in the dish. Repeat with the remaining lasagne strips and filling. Pour the rest of the sauce over the rolls and cover the pan tightly with aluminium foil. Bake the rolls for 20 minutes, then remove the foil and bake them for 15 to 20 minutes more. Serve piping hot.

EDITOR'S NOTE: To compensate for lasagne that may tear during cooking, add one or two extra strips to the boiling water

Vermicelli Salad with Sliced Pork

Serves 6

Working (and total) time: about 30 minutes

Calories 205, Protein 9g, Cholesterol 15mg, Total Fat 3g, Saturated fat 1g, Sodium 235mg

250 g/8 oz	*vermicelli (or other long, thin pasta)*
1/2 tbsp	*safflower oil*
125 g/4 oz	*pork loin, fat trimmed, meat pounded flat and sliced into thin strips*
2	*garlic cloves, finely chopped*
3	*carrots, peeled and julienned*
4	*sticks celery, trimmed and julienned*
2 tsp	*dark sesame oil*
1/4 tsp	*salt*
	freshly ground black pepper
6	*drops Tabasco sauce*
2 tbsp	*rice vinegar*
1 tsp	*sweet sherry*

Break the vermicelli into thirds and drop it into 3 litres (5 pints) of boiling water with 1/2 teaspoons of salt. Start testing the pasta after 5 minutes and continue to cook it until it is *al dente*.

While the pasta is cooking, heat the safflower oil in a wok or a large frying pan over medium-high heat. Stir-fry the pork strips in the oil for 2 minutes. Add the garlic and cook for 30 seconds, stirring constantly to keep it from burning. Add the carrots and celery, and stir-fry the mixture for 2 minutes more.

Drain the pasta and toss it in a large bowl with the pork and vegetable mixture. Dribble the sesame oil over the pasta, then sprinkle it with the 1/4 teaspoon of salt, the black pepper and the Tabasco sauce, and toss thoroughly. Pour the vinegar and sherry over the salad and toss it once more. Serve the salad at room temperature or chilled.

Penne with Smoked Pork and Mushroom Sauce

Serves 8

Working time: about 15 minutes

Total time: about 45 minutes

Calories 315, Protein 11g, Cholesterol 5mg, Total fat 6g, Saturated fat 2g, Sodium 215mg

500 g/1 lb	*penne (or other short, tubular pasta)*
.25 kg/2 1/2 lb	*Italian plum tomatoes, quartered, or 800 g (28 oz) canned whole tomatoes, drained*
4	*whole dried red chilli peppers*
2 tbsp	*virgin olive oil*
1	*onion, finely chopped*
500 g/1 lb	*mushrooms, wiped clean and sliced*
60 g/2 oz	*smoked pork loin or smoked back bacon, julienned*
2.5 cl/4 fl oz	*dry white wine*
2 tbsp	*chopped parsley, preferably flat-leaf*
15 g/1/2 oz	*unsalted butter*

a large saucepan, combine the tomatoes, chilli peppers and 4 tablespoons of water. Cook over medium eat until the tomatoes have rendered their juice and ost of the liquid has evaporated—about 20 minutes. ork the mixture through a sieve and set it aside.

Add the penne to 3 litres (5 pints) of boiling water ith 1 1/2 teaspoons of salt. Begin testing the pasta ter 10 minutes and cook it until it is *al dente*.

While the pasta is cooking, heat the oil in a large ying pan over medium-high heat. Add the onion and ute it, stirring constantly, until it turns translucent—

about 3 minutes. Add the mushrooms and sauté them for 2 minutes, then add the pork and garlic and sauté for 2 minutes more. Pour in the wine and cook the mixture until the liquid is reduced by half—about 3 minutes. Stir in the reserved tomato mixture and the parsley, and keep the sauce warm.

Drain the penne and transfer it to a serving dish. Toss it with the butter and the sauce and serve.

Macaroni Baked with Stilton and Port

Serves 6

Working time: about 20 minutes

Total time: about 45 minutes

Calories 300, Protein 11g, Cholesterol 15mg, Total fat 9g,
Saturated fat 4g, Sodium 400mg

250 g/8 oz	*elbow macaroni*
1 tbsp	*safflower oil*
2	*shallots, finely chopped*
2 tbsp	*flour*
12.5 cl/4 fl oz	*ruby port*
¼ litre/8 fl oz	*semi-skimmed milk*
¼ litre/8 fl oz	*unsalted chicken stock*
125 g/4 oz	*Stilton, crumbled*
2 tsp	*Dijon mustard*
⅛ tsp	*white pepper*
4 tbsp	*dry breadcrumbs*
1 tsp	*paprika*

Preheat the oven to 180°C (350°F or Mark 4). Pour the oil into a large, heavy-bottomed saucepan over medium heat. Add the shallots and cook them, stirring occasionally, until they are transparent—approximately 2 minutes. Sprinkle the flour over the shallots and cook the mixture, stirring continuously, for 2 minutes more.

Pour the port into the pan and whisk slowly; add the milk and the stock in the same manner, whisking after each addition, to form a smooth sauce. Gently simmer the sauce for 3 minutes. Stir in half of the cheese along with the mustard and pepper. Continue stirring until the cheese has melted.

Meanwhile, cook the macaroni in 3 litres (5 pints) of boiling water with 1½ teaspoons of salt. Start testing the pasta after 10 minutes and cook it until it is *al dente*.

Drain the macaroni and combine it with the sauce, then transfer the mixture to a baking dish. Combine the breadcrumbs with the remaining crumbled cheese and scatter the mixture evenly over the top. Sprinkle the paprika over all and bake the dish until the sauce is bubbling hot and the top is crisp—20 to 25 minutes. Serve immediately.